THE END OF THE ROADS

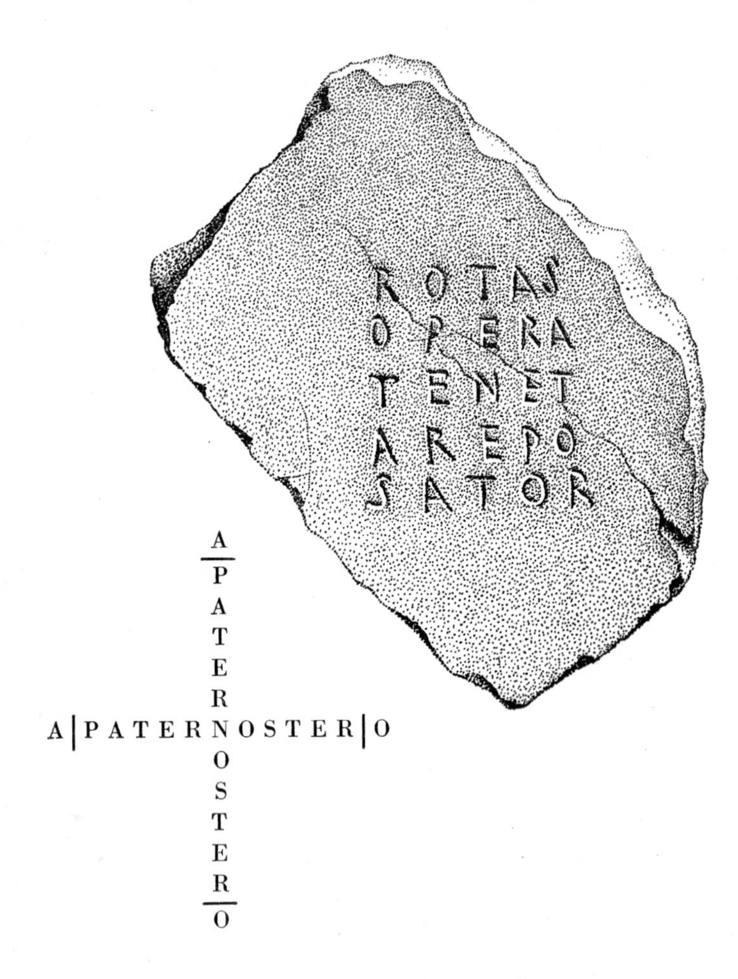

An early Christian puzzle found at Cirencester
With its answer (another puzzle? Look at page 245 f.)

The End
of the
Roads

by
A. F. TITTERTON
and
CATHERINE B. FIRTH

Illustrated by
K. F. ROWLAND

ROADS TO CHRISTIAN FAITH
BOOK FOUR

Ginn and Company Ltd
18 Bedford Row
London WC1

ROADS TO CHRISTIAN FAITH

Editor *Catherine B. Firth*

BOOK ONE

CROSSED KEYS AND CROSSED SWORDS

by Catherine B. Firth

BOOK TWO

ROADS OF ISRAEL

by Catherine B. Firth

BOOK THREE

SERVANTS OF GOD AT WORK

by A. F. Titterton

BOOK FOUR

THE END OF THE ROADS

by A. F. Titterton and C. B. Firth

Second impression 1959

105905

PRINTED IN GREAT BRITAIN BY R. & R. CLARK, LTD., EDINBURGH

To the reader

THIS book is meant specially for people who expect shortly to leave school and go out into world. Before taking that step, while time is given you, it is useful to do some thinking. What are you looking for in life? Where, in the long run, are you going? Where life takes us in the end depends to a great degree upon ourselves, upon what we believe really matters, and so upon what we do.

Nearly three hundred years ago, John Bunyan wrote a 'dream'. It was about a man called Christian who studied the Bible and did some hard thinking. The first result was that he cried out, 'What shall I do?' Then he took advice from one called Evangelist, a teacher of the truth. Now he knew where he really wanted to go. He left his old home, in the city of Destruction, where people lived as they pleased and never thought what would come of it, and set off towards a far-distant light. The king of the land to which he was going had seen that he was provided with good counsellors and a parchment roll, so that he was able to obtain advice and refreshment by the way. This did not mean that the journey was easy. Christian met all kinds of difficulties and dangers. He was tempted by bad counsellors, such as Mr. Worldly Wiseman, to make wrong choices. In the end, though, he reached the Celestial City.

The second part of this book is illustrated by pictures taken from a copy of Bunyan's *Pilgrim's Progress*, which was printed in 1787. The eighteenth-century woodcuts may seem merely funny to some of us today; but so might our illustrations of the story seem to others hundreds of years on. The book has been republished many times over the past three hundred years and in more than a hundred languages. It has been produced with many different kinds of pictures. (You may be asked by your teacher to invent pictures for a modern edition.) Christian, the man of Bunyan's dream, has seemed real to millions of people in different lands and at different times.

Why is this? One reason, we might say, is that so many people have seen in Christian themselves; a man (or a woman) who is unsatisfied with himself and the world around him, who wants to know the road to a better life, who is ready both to struggle and to accept help to reach his goal.

This book is no *Pilgrim's Progress*, but it is intended for boys and girls who want to step off into life on the right foot. In it they are asked to consider three things, or group of things. First, what are we to believe, and why? Secondly, and as a result, what are we to do? Thirdly, what answers can we find to some of the problems of the road which many already may have been turning over in their minds, and for which there is no simple answer?

Many helpers have shared in the making of this book, and Canon Stancliffe has kindly read it in proof. To him, to those whose names are in the Reference Book, and to those whose names are not, the authors are grateful.

A. F. TITTERTON

NEWBURY, BERKS
Whitsuntide 1958

CONTENTS

What are we to believe?

What are we to do?

Puzzles and Paradoxes

ILLUSTRATIONS

PART ONE

What are we to believe?

by

A. F. Titterton

CHAPTER I

Holidays and the Creed

For study

A psalm often read before holidays

Psalm cxxi. 1-3, 7, 8

A psalm used by Jewish pilgrims on holiday

Psalm cxxii

Wisdom's advice

Proverbs viii. 1-5, 11, 32-36

Proverbs ix. 10

For extra reading

This writer valued holy days

Psalm xlii. 1-5

A prayer for perplexed people

Psalm xxv. 4, 5

HOLIDAYS. Why begin a term's work by reminding people of those? Why not? This is a book about the Christian religion. If it had not been for that religion our most important holidays would not be there at all.

Look at the plan on page 16 to see how many public holidays are either holy days themselves or linked with holy days. Before you turn back, try to be quite sure for yourself which days have a connection with some part of the Christian story.

Are all readers sure of these five days?

1	*Christmas Day*	The birth of Jesus
2	Boxing Day	Linked with Christmas rejoicing
3	*Good Friday*	The crucifixion of Jesus
4	Easter Monday	Linked with *Easter Sunday*: the resurrection of Jesus
5	Whit Monday	Linked with *Whit Sunday*: the coming of the Holy Spirit

Some schools have a holiday on Ascension Day, which comes forty days after Easter Sunday. Others have a holiday on a special Saint's Day, perhaps the holy day of the saint whose name the school bears. These holidays are not now public holidays, but there was a time when in a sense they were.

In the Middle Ages there were no Bank holidays nor regular Saturday holidays, no long school holidays. But the Church had more than fifty holy days. On these days workers expected to be free to go to church and then usually to enjoy themselves. So they had on an average one holiday each week, not counting Sundays.

Everyone knew these days. They made a Church calendar, and people were able to date letters by them. A letter might be dated 'Sunday before All Hallow' (before All Saints' Day, November 1st) or 'Bartholomas tide' (round about St. Bartholomew's Day, August 24th). Holy days marked business dates too—and they still do. Look at the table of Quarter Days below. These are days on which, even now, rents are commonly due and fire insurances expire.

QUARTER DAYS

English		*Scottish*	
Lady Day	Mar. 25	Candlemas	Feb. 2
Midsummer Day	June 24	Whitsunday	May 15
(St. John Baptist's Day)		(fixed date used)	
Michaelmas Day	Sept. 29	Lammas	Aug. 1
Christmas Day	Dec. 25	Martinmas	Nov. 11

On *Lady Day* is celebrated the appearance of the Angel Gabriel to the Virgin Mary.

On *Candlemas* is celebrated the occasion when Mary carried the infant Jesus to be dedicated to God in the Temple. On this festival people used to carry candles or torches in procession as some still do in church.

Lammas means loaf-mass, the day on which offerings were made in church of the first-fruits of the harvest.

Readers may notice how many names end with 'mas'. This means the same as 'mass', a name given in some churches to the service of Holy Communion. On each holy day at that service special prayer was offered, appropriate to the day. Most people in the Church of England do not attach the same importance to Saints' days as their ancestors did in the Middle Ages. But if any readers who have books of Common

Prayer look at 'the Calendar with the table of lessons' near the front, they will find all the holy days that have been mentioned in this chapter are there and a great many others besides. Then let them look at the section labelled 'the Collects, Epistles, and Gospels to be used throughout the year'. They will find that some of the most important holy days are shown in their place in the Church year. Other important days are grouped together at the end of the section. There is a special prayer, and special readings from a Gospel and one of the Epistles, for the Communion service on each of these days.

The men who at the time of the Reformation made the first English Prayer Book, took holy days for granted, but they thought that the Catholic Church had attached too much importance to the saints and their powers. In general, in England Saints' days became less important. The people known as Puritans objected to keeping any days at all as special holy days, apart, of course, from Sundays. It was not only that they thought that the services connected with these days were 'superstitious'. They said, too, that holy days were used as an excuse for noisy kinds of fun, of which they disapproved.

Workers' holidays were bound to suffer. Then, as more and more people became employed in city businesses and workshops, there was extra pressure to squeeze the old holidays out. In the eighteenth century, bank clerks still expected bank doors to be closed on forty-seven days in the year. Early in the nineteenth century they still claimed thirty-three days' holiday. Then, suddenly, in 1834, by Act of Parliament, these holidays were reduced to four days. There were the

PUBLIC HOLIDAYS

Two holy days when all banks close

GOOD FRIDAY
CHRISTMAS DAY

—

Bank Holidays

England, Wales, Northern Ireland & Eire, Channel Isles

EASTER MONDAY
WHIT MONDAY
1st MONDAY IN AUGUST
BOXING DAY

—

Scotland

NEW YEAR'S DAY
1st MONDAY IN MAY
1st MONDAY IN AUGUST

—

Northern Ireland & Eire (extra)

ST. PATRICK'S DAY (MARCH 17th)

—

Northern Ireland (extra)

ORANGEMAN'S DAY (JULY 12th)

two great holy days, Christmas and Good Friday, and only two others. Not only bank clerks suffered. The banks were made to open because they were needed for all kinds of business to go on. Business, the bankers and the Government thought, was more important than pleasure. It was at this time, it has been said, that clerks and office-boys began to invent extra grand-mothers, whose funerals had to take place many miles away. But not even the boldest office-boy dared invent important reasons for missing work on more than a few extra days in the year.

Some people became worried because workers had so few holidays. In the nineteenth century, more and more people in shops, factories, and workshops were working for six long days each week. Sunday was a holiday, but respectable people were expected to spend in a quiet way the hours when they were not in church or chapel. Of the four holidays, Good Friday was a solemn day. In the past, many holy days had meant both religion and fun. Now workers had only three 'official' days for fun in the whole year.

At last, in 1871, a man called Lord Avebury managed to get a Bill through Parliament by which banks should be closed each year in England, Wales, and Ireland for four days, not two, apart from Christmas Day and Good Friday. Three of these days were to follow great holy days. That is how we got Boxing Day, Easter Monday, and Whit Monday as holidays. To give workers a late summer break, a fourth day was fixed in August. These four days were called Bank holidays and became general public holidays.

Scottish holidays, readers will have noticed, are a separate group. Turn back again and count them.

There are five, not six, public holidays, and none of the Bank holidays is linked with a holy day. The reason for this lies back in the Reformation too. When in the sixteenth century, Scotsmen made their reformed Church a presbyterian Church, their leaders swept away all holy days. (Though holy days still mark Quarter Days.) Some Scotsmen still preferred, and prefer, a church governed by bishops, an episcopal Church. So in Scotland as well as the National Church, which is presbyterian, there is a Scottish Episcopal Church which has its own Prayer Book and calendar of holy days. But the 'Piskies', as they are often called, cannot expect that their holy days will be also public holidays.

Scottish banks, it was decided, should close on Christmas Day and Good Friday to fit in with English banks. But these days were not counted either holy days or general holidays. When the Act of 1871 was passed, Scotland was given Bank holidays which most Scots preferred, New Year's Day, following Hogmanay, and two other days spaced through the year. This sounds as if Scots would go short on holidays, but, in fact, in Scotland there are local spring and autumn holidays as well. These 'trades holidays' or 'fairs' are not all at the same time. Workers in Edinburgh are free at one time, those in Glasgow at another. Also in recent years far fewer Scots have objected to treating an ancient holy day like Christmas as a public holiday. In fact, many Scottish people now make Christmas a special time of rejoicing both in church and at home.

Scotland had her special reasons for sweeping away Church holidays, but in England and Wales only one of the great public holidays is not directly linked with the Christian religion. That is August Bank holiday.

It is important for something different, something which we might not call religious at all. In whatever part of the British Isles we live, we connect this holiday with our summer holidays. Boys and girls look forward to enjoying themselves out of doors as much as possible. Many hope to spend at least a short time at the sea or in the country. Most people now live in towns and are surrounded by the things which man has made. When their summer holiday comes they get a chance to see more of the world as God makes it. Many readers may remember the special feeling they had when they first caught sight of the sea. Some may know a different feeling, the one people get when they find themselves among lonely hills. There may be plenty of other special rememberings of sea or hills or countryside. So it is possible to think of our August holiday as the festival of God the Creator. Then, if we link each 'English' public holiday in the year with one important statement in our Creed, August Bank holiday will be the 'holy day' connected with the first sentence of all.

Does each reader know the Apostles' Creed? Those who do not can find it, in three parts, on pages 26, 59, 86. A creed is a statement of some of the most important things which people believe. In the Church of England Prayer Book the Apostles' Creed is part of Morning and Evening Prayer. It was not really used by the apostles. It is very ancient, though, more than twelve hundred years old. A creed like this was first recited by people in Rome, in front of the congregation, when they were baptized.

Many of those who read this book were baptized (christened) when they were babies. God-parents 'stood-in' for them, we might say, until they should be old enough to be responsible for their own beliefs. Boys and girls who have reached the age of fourteen, whether they have been baptized or not, are old enough to follow the advice of Wisdom in the book of Proverbs. They can 'get understanding' for themselves. Each sentence of the Creed is a flat summary of something which Christians see as urgently important. Why urgently? In this term's work readers can discover for themselves some of the answers. They can see, too, how the events in the Christian story matter so much to believers that they are glad to celebrate them by Holy Days—and holidays.

CHAPTER II

Believing in God the Creator

For study

God invisible

1 Timothy vi. 16

1 John iv. 12, 13

God beyond all

1 Kings viii. 22-23 and 27

Isaiah lxvi. 1, 2

Isaiah lvii 15

Psalm xc. 1, 2 and 4

Psalm cii. 24-27

For extra reading

God the creator of all things

Psalm civ. 1-5, 10-14

Job xi. 1, 7, 8

Job xii. 1, 2, 7-10

'I BELIEVE in God . . . maker of heaven and earth.' Do you? Some readers will say, 'Yes, of course'. Others may say, 'Yes, I suppose so'. Others, again, may say, 'I am not so sure'.

Well, why? Suppose, before reading further, each writes down all the reasons he or she can think of why people should believe in God the Creator, or their reasons for not believing in him.

Here are reasons which some people may give for believing. One may say, 'I believe because I have been taught about God by people (at school, or church, or home) who know what they are talking about'. Another may say, 'I believe because it is in the Bible'. A third reason for believing may be because of beautiful or mysterious things which a person has seen or enjoyed: these things seem to be explained best as coming from God, as his work. All these reasons are good ones, and there may be others.

Someone here may say, 'But even if you believe in God, you can't believe what the Bible says about God making the world in seven days'. There is no need to read the Creation story in Genesis that way. Readers of *Roads of Israel* have already thought about its picture of God the Creator working in 'days'. These are poetic 'days', long periods of time. A psalmist once wrote of God:

. . . a thousand years in thy sight are but as yesterday when it is past, and as a watch [a few hours] in the night.

A very late stage (or day) was the making of man.

Now, as to those people who are not so certain. One may say, 'How can anyone be sure about God? No-one has seen him.' Or, 'If he made us, who made God?' Another may say, 'People don't believe in God nowadays. They believe in science.' Yet another may say, 'God can't be the kind of person the Bible says he is, or he would not let so many horrible things happen'.

The last answer does not belong to this chapter, but to a later one. The others can be looked at now.

'No-one has seen God.' That is true. It has been said or sung many times. The writer of the first Epistle to Timothy expressed it this way, 'his [God's] dwelling is in unapproachable light; no human eye has seen or can ever see him'. In church people sing:

> Immortal, invisible, God only wise,
> In light inaccessible, hid from our eyes.

When you come to think of it, how would you expect to be able to see, just like that, the creator of this immense universe? Some readers can point out the Milky Way in the sky. That one galaxy, as it is called, of stars consists of one hundred thousand million stars (100,000,000,000). To grasp even the size of the universe is quite beyond our minds. How could we 'see' its creator? Yet if not, how can we be sure about him?

This is where the Christian answer comes in. Because we men can best understand that way, God sent Jesus Christ, both God and man, into the world to show us what he himself is like. In the first chapter of St. John's Gospel you can find these words:

> No man hath seen God at any time; the only begotten Son [Jesus Christ] . . . he hath declared him [made him clear to us].

'Who made God?' Why should anybody make him? We ask the question, 'Who made God?' because we live in a world of created things. Shakespeare said that life is like a stage and we the players on that stage. Like actors, we occupy our stage only for a certain time. Everything we do, we do at a certain place at a certain time. You can't get away from that! A great scientist called Einstein showed, by mathematics too difficult for ordinary people to understand, that there is no space without time, or time without space. There is only space-time. Does that make the reader's head spin? In the universe in which we find ourselves, everything takes place in space-time, on the great stage, as it were. God, the Creator, belongs to eternity, beyond space and time.

> I saw Eternity the other night,
> Like a great ring of pure and endless light,
> All calm, as it was bright;
> And round beneath it, Time in hours, days, years,
> Driven by the spheres
> Like a vast shadow mov'd; in which the world
> And all her train were hurl'd.

That is how an English poet three hundred years ago saw eternity and time. Some readers may see no sense in his vision. They may prefer the words in which a Bible poet explained that God is eternal:

> Before the mountains were brought forth, or ever thou hadst formed the earth and the world, even from everlasting to everlasting, thou art God.

Later, the man who wrote the first Epistle to Timothy showed God beyond space and time when he said, 'he is King of Kings and Lord of Lords; to him only immortality [for-everness, or never-dyingness] belongs'.

'People believe in science.' The business of a scientist is not to say who made the world, but what the world is made of and how it works. Scientists, especially during the last three hundred years, have found out more and more about this. They make one experiment after another and try to find out 'laws', as they say, according to which all created things exist and change.

The men who in the seventeenth century founded modern science were Christians. They took for granted that God made the world, so of course there was sense in it. They were interested to find out more about the universe and the whole pattern of things. A famous scientist, Galileo, an Italian, invented a telescope with which he could study the stars. One thing became clear to him: the earth is only a small planet which moves round the sun. Many people who heard this were shocked. They said that it was part of the Christian religion to believe that God had made the world the centre of the universe and man the lord of the world. Galileo could not see what they had to worry about. His discovery did not prevent him from believing in God and Christ. It took many other Christians, though, quite a long time to get used to the new point of view.

Some of us may sympathize with these people. It makes us uncomfortable to think of millions and millions of stars in almost limitless space. (To take a space ship and explore one or two of the nearest planets might be an adventure.) If this is what science shows us, can we really believe that there is any good in having a religion at all—that we can matter to the Creator? Our

I believe in God the Father Almighty,
Maker of heaven and earth:

feeling is not a new one. Men shared it long before the coming of modern science. A psalmist said to God:

> When I consider thy heavens, the work of thy fingers, the moon and the stars which thou hast ordained; what is man that thou art mindful of him? and the son of man, that thou visitest him?

The psalmist, though, did not stop there. He was not, like Galileo, a Christian, for Christ had not yet come into the world. But somehow he was quite sure that God is mindful of man, so he went on:

> Thou hast made him [man] a little lower than the angels, and hast crowned him with glory and honour. Thou madest him to have dominion over the works of thy hands; thou hast put all things under his feet.

Jesus Christ put God's mindfulness of man in a more homely way when he said:

> Are not two sparrows sold for a farthing? and one of them shall not fall on the ground without your Father . . .
>
> Fear ye not therefore; ye are of more value than many sparrows.

Today there are a number of scientists, as there are a number of other people, who would say that they cannot be sure themselves that the psalmist or even Jesus Christ was right. But these men still write all the time as if they expect the world to be not a chance jumble of things but created in a reasonable way. A scientist, Sir James Jeans, some years ago, in a book called *The Mysterious Universe*, said that it seemed to him that God must have been very, very good at mathematics. Again, it is said, to understand creation you must understand other kinds of science, since the whole of creation is made up of energy. Our Creator, from the scientist's point of view, must be a genius at all the sciences.

Here some readers may wish to interrupt. 'This is very dull. You can't tie God down to being a glorified kind of scientist. How about beautiful things? They tell you more about God than all these experiments. But you can't weigh beauty, or take its temperature either.' That is quite true, and another thing you can't weigh or measure is goodness. You simply can't get a 'flat' picture of God or of his works. The scientist, Jeans, was right. We live in a mysterious universe. Verses set *For study* show some ways in which people have said this. Readers may know poems which have expressed it in other ways.

One verse set for reading is part of a prayer which we know as King Solomon's prayer at the dedication of his Temple. The king asks:

> Will God indeed dwell on the earth? behold the heaven and heaven of heavens cannot contain thee; how much less this house that I have builded?

What is meant by 'heaven' or 'heavens' here? When we speak of God maker of heaven or the heavens we can mean two different things. Perhaps the writer of the prayer had both in mind. The first is that God is the maker of the immensity of space in which millions of stars take their course. The second is that God is the creator of the unseen universe, off our stage, as it were, the home of angels and spirits. There God, says Isaiah, dwells with people of a humble spirit. Jesus called these people children of the Kingdom of Heaven.

CHAPTER III

Believing in God the Father

For study

Prayer

Matthew vi. 9-15

Luke xi. 1-4, 9-13

The Prodigal Son

Luke xv. 11-32

For extra reading

Care for children and the lost

Matthew xviii. 1-4, 10-14

'I believe in God the Father Almighty.' These words must sound quite natural to most readers, though perhaps they could not say why. In fact, ever since they were small children they have said the prayer which Jesus taught his disciples, beginning 'Our Father which art in heaven'. From the Gospels we can see that Jesus counted God as his father from the time when he was a boy. Readers may recall his reply to his mother when she found him in the Temple (Luke ii. 49). When he spoke to God he called him Father; and he taught his disciples to think of God in that way.

Now if readers were asked what they thought a perfect father should be like, they would not all have the same ideas. Some of them would most want a father whom they can respect, who can be stern with those who do wrong, as well as gentle at the right time. But others might prefer one who makes you his special favourite or who gives you all that you want, the spoiling kind.

If we think through the Lord's Prayer we can see to which kind of father Jesus taught us to pray. Here is the prayer in an unusual version:

Our Father in heaven,
thy name be revered,
thy Reign begin,
thy will be done
on earth as in heaven!

This clearly means that God is a Father whom we wish to be honoured and obeyed. The prayer goes on:

Give us today our bread for the morrow,
And forgive us our debts
  as we ourselves have forgiven our debtors,
And lead us not into temptation,
  but deliver us from evil.

We ask our Father to care for us, to forgive us our faults and to keep us from things that are too hard for us. The whole picture is of the first kind of father.

Jesus taught that his Father the Creator has a care for all his children, good and bad (look at Matthew v. 45). Sun and rain, the chance to sow and to reap, are given to all. It might even seem on the surface from some of Jesus' stories that if God does have favourites, they are the bad boys, the people who have made a mess of things. One of these stories is that of the Prodigal (wasteful) Son, which many people know.

The prodigal son was the younger of two brothers. He knew that when his father died, or perhaps when the father became too old to look after things properly himself, his property would be divided and each son would get a share. The younger son wanted to be free to carry on his own life. He came to his father and asked to have his share of the property now. The father took a big risk. He divided the property. According to Jewish custom he gave the younger son his share (one-third) and the elder son his share (two-thirds). Some time afterwards the younger son sold his share of the family land and sheep and cattle, and went off to have what he hoped would be a good time. When he had spent his fortune on drink and girls and gambling, there was a famine. Prices shot up, his money was spent and he ended by doing work which Jews regarded as unclean—he became a swine-herd. He was glad to eat the 'husks' which were fed to the pigs. They were pods of the carob tree and only used for food by the poorest people.

Now the father had not spoiled the son at home. He had simply left him free to spoil himself if he meant to do so. The young man had had the same ideas as thousands of other people—that if you can get hold of money and a chance for travel and a gay time you are bound to be happy. He found that things did not work out that way. (So much for the people who believe that if God would only hand them out everything they want how happy they would be!) As it was, a big dose of hardship brought him to his senses. He 'came to himself', and he thought about home. He knew that there even the hired servants had plenty to eat, and here was he starving. He decided that he had done wrong. He would go back, apologize to his father, and ask him to take him on as a servant.

The young man went home. His father saw him while he was still a long way off and ran out to greet him affectionately. The son managed to get out his apology, but he never got so far as to ask if he might be a servant: he was already being treated as a son, one restored, as it were, from the dead.

The elder brother was out on the farm. Probably he despised his younger brother and was resentful that he had lost family property. He himself, so he thought, knew how to behave if his younger brother did not. Though he had received his share of the property and worked the farm, he still treated his father as head of the family. Today, as this elder brother came back from work, when he got near the house he heard music and dancing. A servant explained that his younger brother had returned and his father had ordered the fattened calf to be killed, the one that was ready against the coming of an honoured guest.

The elder brother was furious. He refused to go in. His father came out to entreat him to share in the rejoicing. But the son pointed out that for years he had stayed on the land and worked for his father, yet he had never even been offered a kid, to make a good supper for his friends. Now, as soon as his younger brother, that wastrel, came home, the fattened calf was killed in his honour. The father saw the matter differently. He explained that his elder son was his constant companion. Everything of his father's was his already. It was proper to be glad when the 'lost' brother came home.

The father has no favourite, but the son who was lost to him is found again. The elder brother is respectable and hard-working, but he does not know when he is well off. All the time that his brother has been away he has been by his father's side, helping to make the home prosper. Of course he has to work hard, but hard work is good for healthy people. He probably meets danger at times from lions or bears, prowling after the farm stock; but he has his sling and bludgeon, and a spice of danger makes life more interesting. His trouble is that he is proud and ungenerous. So he spoils things for himself as well as for his brother, and stays outside the party.

The bad boy has got himself into the trouble he deserved. He has seen that he must be prepared to suffer for his foolishness all his life. Because he shows himself of 'a contrite and humble spirit' he comes nearer to his father than the elder brother. (Pride has a way of separating people both from each other and from God.)

In the story of the Prodigal Son, the well-behaved brother prospered in this world. The badly-behaved one did not. He got, at first, what he deserved. But, as readers may point out, life does not always work out like that. Sometimes it seems that people suffer terribly who are not only hard-working but all sorts of other good things too. Meanwhile many unpleasant people get on and have a good time. Then some of us are liable to say, 'How unfair. Can God really be a father of the kind that Jesus Christ says he is, if he lets these things happen?' This is an old, old puzzle. A whole book in the Bible consists of a kind of play with this puzzle as its plot.

CHAPTER IV

Job questions God

For study

Job's two trials

Job i. 8-22

Job ii. 3-10

Some questions to Job

Job xxxviii. 1-7, 16-18, 22, 25-27, 39-41

The Epilogue

Job xlii. 10-17

For extra reading

Well-known verses

Job v. 6, 7

Job ix. 25, 26

('post' means a swift messenger)

Job xiv. 1, 2

Job xxiii. 3, 10

('he' means God)

More questions

Job xxxix. 13-20, 26-27

THE book of Job tells how God allowed Satan to test a man who was one of God's servants. In your Bible the story probably appears in prose. In Hebrew there is a Prologue, which is mostly prose, and a prose Epilogue, but the rest of the book is written in poetry. In this account of the story most of the quotations are taken from a version which shows the poetic form.

Readers will find that the book is quite a long one. But chapters xxxii to xxxvii, where a young man called Elihu comes in and makes long speeches, were probably put in later. No quotations are given from these chapters. Descriptions of two great animals, the elephant and the crocodile, were also, it is thought, added later. They are interesting, but not part of the play.

This is the story. There was a man in the land of Uz called Job. He was one who feared God and tried to do right. God blessed him with seven sons and three daughters, and he was a good father to them. Job was a wealthy farmer. He had 7000 sheep and 3000 camels and 500 yoke of oxen and 500 she-asses, besides a great household of servants.

A day came when the guardian spirits of man came to present themselves before God. One, Satan, whose job was to test mankind, was among them. Satan told God that Job only served him because God was so good to him. He said that God had only to rob Job of everything that he had and Job would turn against him.

God told Satan that he might have power over all that belonged to Job, but he must not touch Job himself. So Satan went forth from God's presence. Soon afterwards, while Job's children were all feasting in the eldest brother's house, messengers came one by one to Job. The first said:

The oxen were ploughing,
  and the asses feeding beside them;
and the Sabeans fell upon them,
  and took them away;
Yea, they have slain thy servants with the edge of the sword;
and I only am escaped alone to tell thee!

Three more messengers came. Find out from Job i, verses 16 to 19, the news that each brought. In the end, you will see, Job had lost almost all.

Job arose. He tore his mantle and shaved his head in sign of grief. He fell to the ground and worshipped God and said that he came into the world with nothing, he would leave it with nothing:

> The Lord gave, and the Lord hath taken away:
> Blessed be the Name of the Lord.

Job, at least in words, had accepted God's will.

When a second time the guardian spirits assembled, God pointed out how well his servant Job had behaved. But Satan was not content. He told God that a man would give anything to preserve his life. If God would make Job suffer in his own body, Job would soon turn against him. God said that Satan might make Job suffer, but he must spare his life.

So Satan went forth and caused Job to be covered all over with horrible, oozing boils. Even his wife said at this point that he would do best to turn against God and die. But Job replied, 'What?, shall we receive good at the hand of God, and shall we not receive evil?'

Again from his words it seemed as if he believed it was right to accept what God sends without a murmur.

Now Job was a man who was used to life at the edge of the desert. Desert dwellers, like sailors, often have a great respect for God. Looking up into the vast sky, or over miles and miles of mountains or plains, they know how small and helpless they are. Tempests, drought, dust-storms, can overwhelm men and their flocks and herds. It is easy to die alone, of thirst or of hunger. That is one reason why many desert people in later years accepted the teaching of Mohammed. (He was a camel-driver in the desert about A.D. 600.) Mohammed was sure that all that comes to us is from Allah (his name for God) the Compassionate, the Merciful. We are in his hands. Our duty is to submit to his will. So Mohammed's religion is often called Islam which means 'submission'.

Job could not easily submit without question. As a Jew, he had been taught that God is righteous. Though Job had said in words that he accepted God's will, he could not see why a righteous God should treat him so unkindly when he had always served him faithfully. Job felt so utterly miserable that he cursed the day that he was born. If only he had died that very day:

> For now should I have lien down and been quiet. . . .
> There the wicked cease from troubling;
> and there the weary be at rest. . . .
> I am not at ease, neither am I quiet,
> Neither have I rest, but trouble cometh!

Now three friends had come to condole with Job over his troubles, and they were shocked by the way he spoke. They all tried to give him good advice. Some of their arguments were ones he might have used earlier himself, about other people's troubles. Now Job felt rather, perhaps, as you would if you sat in church with raging toothache, and someone in the pulpit preached a sermon all about it and you, explaining why you should not grumble!

The first friend, whose name was Eliphaz, pointed out to Job that earlier he had given other people good advice, but now he was suffering himself he was unhappy. Job, he said, was sure that he had not done wrong, but that was saying too much. Eliphaz asked:

> Shall mortal man be just before God?
> Shall a man be pure before his Maker?

He told Job that he should be grateful for his punishment:

> Behold, happy is the man whom God correcteth:
> Therefore despise not thou the chastening of the Almighty.

But Job could find no comfort in what Eliphaz said. He asked God to put an end to his sufferings and let him alone so that he might die.

The second friend, Bildad, then spoke and told Job that he ought not to speak as if God were not fair.

> God will not cast away a perfect man,
> Neither will he uphold the evil-doers.

But Bildad's speech gave Job less help still. God, it seemed, all-knowing and all-powerful, never gave him a chance, never let him alone. Though Job gave him reverence, God followed him up with trouble all the time. It was all the same, Job said, good or bad, God destroyed both the perfect and the wicked. Then Job turned upon God and said:

> Are not my days few?
> Cease then and let me alone,
> That I may take comfort a little,
> Before I go whence I shall not return.

Job's third friend, Zophar, next spoke. He told Job that he ought not to be so sure that he was perfect as God would see perfection. The perfection of God was higher and deeper than he could understand.

> Canst thou by searching find out God?
> Canst thou find out the Almighty unto perfection?

Job found Zophar no more help than the others. He pointed out that his friends might be wisdom itself, but he had as much understanding as they. He knew as well as they did what God is like. He knew that God is just and wise. But he was still certain that he was suffering like a wicked man, though he had not done wrong. If only God would take away all this frightfulness and listen to what he had to say and explain things to him himself. There was a moment when he really knew that one day, after death, God would make all clear to him; but later, in his need, he cried:

> Oh, that I knew where I might find him [God],
> That I might come even to his seat!

Nothing that his friends, those 'miserable comforters' as he called them, could say was any help.

Finally Job stood up and swore before God that he had never broken God's law in any one thing. He went through all his good deeds. He had never cheated. He had treated his servants justly. He had cared for the poor and widows and orphans. He had never been a miser or one that tried to get hold of other people's property. He had always been hospitable to strangers. If he had done any wrong, then let God punish him.

There Job stood, one man, his hands raised, pointing out his little virtues to God, asking for justice. When he had uttered his oath he found that he was in the midst of a storm. Out of the storm he seemed to hear God's voice asking:

Who is this that darkeneth counsel by words without knowledge?
[Who is this who makes God's plans seem unwise by talking of what he doesn't understand?]
Gird now up thy loins [prepare for work] like a man;
For I will demand of thee, and declare thou unto me.
Where wast thou when I laid the foundations of the earth?
—Declare if thou hast understanding . . .
Hast thou commanded the morning since thy days began,
And caused the dayspring to know its place? . . .
Hast thou entered into the springs of the sea?
Or hast thou walked in the recesses of the deep?

Question after question came to Job. Readers can find them in chapters xxxviii and xxxix. What did Job know about the mysteries of God's creation? Could he make or guide the world and the host of stars himself? What did he know even of the nature of the beasts and birds which God had made and supplied with their food?

Finally God asked if the person who was struggling with him had now seen his mistake. God ordered the man who had been arguing with him to answer.

Job was feeling very small. He said:

Behold I am of small account; what shall I answer thee?
I lay mine hand upon my mouth.

Soon God repeated the order:

> Gird up thy loins now like a man:
> I will demand of thee, and declare thou unto me.

This time Job was asked, 'Was he always going to criticize God, so as to show himself in the right?' Deck yourself, he was told, with dignity and honour and majesty. Look on all proud and wicked men and bring them to punishment. Only then will God count you as someone whose own right hand can save him, who owes nothing to God.

Job was feeling smaller still. This is how the play ends:

JOB (*to God*): I know that thou canst do all things, and that no purpose of thine can be restrained.
VOICE OF GOD (*in the distance, as the storm ends*): Who is this that hideth counsel without knowledge?
JOB (*goes on*): Therefore have I uttered that which I understood not,
Things too wonderful for me, which I knew not.
Hear, I beseech thee and I will speak.
VOICE (*fainter still*): I will demand of thee, and declare thou unto me.
JOB: I had heard of thee by the hearing of the ear;
But now mine eye seeth thee,
Wherefore I abhor [hate] myself, and repent
In dust and ashes.

The trial was over. Job had started with a high opinion of himself and a belief, usual among Jews, that his Creator would bless him. God had allowed Satan to apply very hard tests but he knew that Job honestly wanted to serve him. He, the Almighty, spoke with Job and left him feeling remarkably humble.

What about the Epilogue? Readers will find that once the trial was over God was kind to his servant Job in a way that he and his neighbours could understand. The friends who had lectured him were shown their foolishness. They went to Job carrying sacrifices which he might offer to God for them; and Job prayed for them. Read the cheerful end to the story in Job xlii, verses 10-16. Some readers may think that this makes a good ending to the play—a 'happy ever after' ending. At the same time they may think that in real life God might not have made up to Job for his troubles in quite so obvious a way. They will be right. The ending is not needed. Job had 'seen' God.

CHAPTER V

Jesus Christ the Bridge

For study

Sacrifice at Shiloh

1 Samuel ii. 13-15

Sacrifice—or service?

Isaiah i. 11-20

Christ the Mediator

Hebrews vii. 19, 26-27
Hebrews viii. 4-12

For extra reading

Light and darkness

1 John i. 5-10

Another prophet on sacrifice and service

Micah vi. 6-8

THE prodigal son of the Gospel story as a young man made no attempt to be good. He was just plain selfish and out to enjoy himself. His elder brother seemed a more worthy man, but he slipped up in the end and showed that underneath he was hard and ungenerous. Job, in the Old Testament story, made great efforts to keep God's laws. To his children he was a kind father, to his servants a just master. Widows and orphans, needy people and strangers, could all rely on him for help and shelter. But Job slipped up too. He tried to be righteous and ended by doubting the goodness of God. Surely he must be unfair, Job felt, if he let people like himself suffer so.

None of us, certainly, is in Job's place. We all know that time and again we do, or say, or think things that are wrong. This worries some people much more than others; but whether it worries them or not, it is true. It used to worry some people in Israel. Moses, as readers of Books Two and Three learned, had shown them that the God who brought them through the desert to the promised land, Canaan, made laws of right living, and they ought to keep those laws. In Canaan many of them had their minds confused. The Canaanites did not know so much about right living. In religion they were what boys and girls of today might call superstitious. They believed that each part of the land was owned by a spirit or spirits, a 'baal'. If they annoyed these gods of the land, they might get into trouble. So they tried to please the 'baals' with sacrifices, presents of the best things which they produced. Two kinds of sacrifice were usual. At times an animal was slain and the whole of its flesh offered to the god. Perhaps more often the 'richest' part of the animal, including much of the fat, was offered to the god. The god's share was burnt, and rose, as the people believed, in smoke to the god. Part was given to the priests who carried out the sacrifice. The worshippers ate the rest at a special meal. They hoped that in sharing the animal's life with the god they would be brought closer to him.

In Canaan the people of Israel had arrangements for regular sacrifices to God, rather after the fashion of the Canaanites. Readers of *Servants of God at Work* may remember how Samuel's parents were among those who came to Shiloh to offer an animal sacrifice. Eli's sons, who were priests, interfered at the time of sacrifice. Who can discover from reading 1 Samuel ii. 13-15 which of the two kinds of sacrifice it was? Later, Elijah was furious with the way so many people neglected God and gave honour to the baals. He believed that God had held back rain for years because of this. The Lord God, he said, controlled nature, not those gods, those baals, of whom images were made.

Later still, the prophet Isaiah watched the processions which came to the great altar of sacrifice before the Temple in Jerusalem. He too was filled with anger. He believed that the people of Israel knew better than to think that this was the way to please the Lord, the Holy One. Read what Isaiah had to say in the book of Isaiah, chapter i, verses 11 to 20. (Readers of Book Three have studied these verses already.) God, he said, had no use for their sacrifices or their prayers, for they had blood on their hands. He meant by this that they had broken the laws of God which they knew. They had been dishonest in their lives and in business. They had taken advantage of poorer people and widows and orphans. Instead of siding with the weak, they had got on at other people's expense. Then they came offering sacrifices to God and thinking that would put all right. What an idea they had of God! They must change their ways, he said, or God would cause them to suffer.

Perhaps some readers may say, 'Well, anyway, I would not behave like that myself'. Perhaps not, but most of us know that though we would not do those particular things, there are other less showy ways in which we do wrong. What is to be done about it?

No one expects to offer a sacrifice to God to take away his anger. Quite a number of people, though, may find themselves trying to make private bargains with him—'O God, if you'll let me off this time and keep Dad from being angry, I promise to be good all next week'. That is not much better. There are other things that we may do. We can apologize to God in a prayer. If we have behaved badly to another person we can try to make amends. That may include apologizing to that person, a most uncomfortable thing to do, if you do it sincerely. (It is easy enough sometimes to snap out 'Sorry'!) But are these things enough?

People of many lands have asked that question again and again. Usually the answer given by their religion is, 'No, you must do more than that'. Amy Carmichael (see *Servants of God at Work*) described in one of her books how she joined with Hindu people who were bathing in a sacred waterfall. Some of them had come on foot for many, many miles. They had been told that if they bathed there they would wash away their sins. A group of the women were widows. They had been

Grant to us, Lord, we beseech thee, the spirit to think and do always such things as be rightful; that we, who cannot do anything that is good without thee, may by thee be enabled to live according to thy will; through Jesus Christ our Lord.

Amen.

taught that it was because of their sins that their husbands died. For years some of them had tried to make up for those sins by eating very little food, and that only of the coarsest kind. One old, grey-haired widow entered the gallery below the waterfall and sat patiently under the pounding water, praying to be made clean. At the end, Amy gave the old widow a hand to help her up. Amy had prayed her own prayer in the words of a psalm, 'O send forth thy light and thy truth, let them lead her'. Now the old woman moved on to finish her ceremony of cleansing, so Amy could not do what she wanted, tell her the Christian answer to her search. The Christian answer, Amy knew, is that you cannot do anything yourself to wash away your sins. You have to leave that to God. It is there that Jesus Christ comes in, bridging the gap between ourselves and God the Creator, the perfect, the holy.

When a man and woman get married, they use a ring as a sign of the bond between them. In Old Testament times when two people made a covenant or agreement, they might slay an animal. The sacrifice was halved, the two parts were placed on the ground, and each of the people making the covenant passed between them. The animal by the giving of its life provided a bridge between the two. It was a mediator. Jesus Christ, 'a priest for ever', as we read in the Epistle to the Hebrews, offered his life to be the mediator of a new testament (or agreement) between God and men. He bridged the gap.

CHAPTER VI

Believing in Jesus Christ

For study

The first Christmas
Luke ii. 1-7, 8-16

A prophet speaks of Bethlehem
Micah v. 2

The Wise Men
Matthew ii. 1-12

For extra reading

Jesus, God's thought for us
John i. 1-5, 10-14

Christians find Jesus here
Isaiah ix. 2, 6, 7

THREE great holy days are directly concerned with Jesus Christ. The first is Christmas.

The Christmas message, so St. Luke tells us, was first sung by angels. For many hundreds of years it has been sung by men and women, girls and boys, in Christmas carols and hymns. To carol once meant to dance in a ring. Later the name carol came to be used for the merry songs sung in honour of Christmas.

Before going further, suppose each reader thinks out the first lines—if possible—of six Christmas hymns or carols, and writes them down. What is the story with which they are concerned? Surely the central part may be found in words such as these:

> Once in royal David's city
> Stood a lowly cattle-shed,
> Where a mother laid her baby
> In a manger for his bed;
> Mary was that mother mild,
> Jesus Christ her little child.

'Royal David's city' was, of course, Bethlehem, the native city of King David. The name Jesus which was given to the baby was quite a common one, though it means Saviour. Many hopeful Jewish parents gave the name to their infant sons. But this Jesus was different from the others, for he was in fact the Christ, the anointed one, the Messiah for whom the Jews had been waiting. (See *Servants of God at Work*, page 120.) They looked for the Messiah to be a 'Son of David', and the family into which he was born was descended from

King David, though his mother Mary was a peasant girl, and he was born in the stable of a crowded inn.

The Messiah, so most Jews believed, was to be their leader in an earthly struggle. It was to be a struggle against the Romans who had conquered them, a struggle to bring in a time of peace and plenty. But this is not the way that Christians see Christ. The hymn quoted above goes on:

> He came down to earth from heaven
> Who is God and Lord of all,

and readers are certain to have on their lists hymns which tell of the message brought to the shepherds that night, the glad tidings that the child was a saviour in a special sense. 'While shepherds watched' is one of these hymns. Another, an ancient carol, not so well known, contains the verse:

> Then God sent an angel from Heaven so high,
> To certain poor shepherds in fields where they lie,
> And bade them no longer in sorrow to stay,
> Because that our Saviour was born on this day.

To the shepherds on the stony hills, away from all the clamour of the crowd, it was made known that among those crowded that night in the little city below was a tiny baby who was special to God, special to man. Who remembers in which hymn these words are found?—

> Veiled in flesh the Godhead see!
> Hail, the incarnate Deity!

Incarnate means in the flesh, or in the body of a man; deity means god. In Jesus, we hail God made man. Here is a description from another hymn:

Word of the Father,
Now in flesh appearing.

Word here means thought, but thought of two kinds, thought in God's mind and thought in action. A boy or girl of today might say, 'When I got back home after the exam, the fire was lit and tea was on the table. It was like Mum's thought.' The coming of Jesus Christ was God's thought for us, shown in a special action. St. John's Gospel explains in its first chapter how God's thought for us was there all the time. Then Christ came. The Jews did not recognize who he was, the true Messiah. They could not receive him. But those who receive him, those who believe in him, can become God's sons.

Another name given to Christ is Emmanuel. This means 'God with us'. Isaiah used it as the name of a coming king. It is a name used for Christ in the prayer which ends the hymn 'O little town of Bethlehem':

We hear the Christmas Angels
The great glad tidings tell:
O come to us, abide with us,
Our Lord Emmanuel.

Some carols on readers' lists may refer to the story told by St. Matthew about the Wise Men. These carols really belong to the last of the twelve days which are given to honouring Christmas—Twelfth Night. This is also called the feast of the Epiphany. The word Epiphany is a Greek one and means a showing. In the Book of Common Prayer the Epiphany is called also the Manifestation (showing) of Christ to the Gentiles. The first Gentiles (strangers) to see the infant Christ were the Wise Men.

Who were they? They were not really kings, though we sing 'We three kings of Orient are'. They were probably astrologers from Babylon or Persia. Astrology was a science of that time, a study of the stars. It was different from modern astronomy. The astronomer, besides plotting the stars and their courses, is interested in their make-up, their chemistry as it were. The astrologer had a more magical interest in the stars. He believed that he could read from their changing patterns the fortunes of men. At the birth of great men there were, in his view, special signs among the stars. Round about the time when Christ was born, the Jews scattered through eastern lands were talking of a coming king. In the years 7 and 6 B.C., it seems, there were unusual groupings of the planets Jupiter, Saturn, and Mars. Afterwards there appeared for a time a single, brilliant star. This was probably the star of the Wise Men. They believed that it heralded the birth of the king of the Jews. They took a long journey by mountain and desert to Jerusalem to give honour to this king. Students now believe that the date of the birth of Christ was not A.D. 1 but 6 B.C. In other words, Christ was born six years earlier than has been thought.

The meaning of the story is clear. The most learned men of their time came many, many miles to seek a king. They ended by laying their gifts at the cradle of Mary's son.

'How can we know what God is like?' people ask. Christians reply that on one special day, nearly two thousand years ago, he sent Jesus Christ into the world to show us. So important was that 'showing' that we celebrate it each year. Jesus Christ in his life and death, as we can see from the Gospels, showed how much God cares for us. Suppose he had showed that God is just a stern judge, waiting to punish us, would Christmas be the same? We all know what life is like when Christmas is in the air. Many people are far nicer then than at any other time. They feel happy, glad to make other people happy. Why? They may not know it, but really it is because, in the words of the old carol, the message is going round:

> God rest you merry, Gentlemen.
> Let nothing you dismay,
> For Jesus Christ our Saviour
> Was born upon this day,
> To save us all from Satan's power
> When we were gone astray:
> O tidings of comfort and joy!

Among the verses set *For study*, there is one from the prophet Micah. Those who have read *Servants of God at Work* will remember how prophets glimpsed, time and again, the coming of a Messiah, a Prince of Peace. The verse set for reading from the prophet Micah was quoted by the writer of St. Matthew's Gospel in his story of the Wise Men. This Gospel was written specially for the Jews, and the writer wanted to show them that Jesus was the Messiah for whom they had been waiting. Most of the Christmas stories are found in St. Luke's Gospel. There are none in the Gospel according to St. Mark. St. John tells no Christmas stories either, but shows Jesus Christ as God's Word.

CHAPTER VII

Good Friday (two weeks)

For study

(*a*) JESUS CHRIST OUR LORD SUFFERED

The cost of 'eternal life'

Mark x. 17-22

Defying the Pharisees

Matthew xxiii. 25, 26
Matthew xii. 9-14

(*b*) OUR LORD SUFFERED UNDER PONTIUS PILATE, WAS CRUCIFIED

One unpopular parable

Mark xii. 1-9

The cross

Matthew xxvii. 24-26, 39-43

For extra reading

(*a*) *Care for all*

Matthew xv. 29-39

(*b*) *The new covenant*

Luke xxii. 14, 15, 19, 20

(*a*) JESUS CHRIST OUR LORD SUFFERED

THE carol quoted on page 55 says that Jesus Christ was born,

> To save us all from Satan's power
> When we were gone astray.

How did he do it? How can he do it? What has suffering to do with the question? The writer of the Epistle to the Hebrews, as Chapter V showed, explained it in one way. His Jewish hearers understood that way, but it is not one that most people today so easily understand.

Jesus liked people to be well and happy. An old carol called 'Joys Seven' very naturally begins:

> The first good joy that Mary had,
> It was the joy of one;
> To see the blessèd Jesus Christ
> When he was first her son.

But it goes on:

> The next good joy that Mary had,
> It was the joy of two;
> To see her own son, Jesus Christ,
> To make the lame to go.
>
> The next good joy that Mary had,
> It was the joy of three;
> To see her own son, Jesus Christ,
> To make the blind to see.

Suppose at this point readers stop and jot down a list of stories which they remember about works of healing which Jesus did. Can they find ten different kinds of trouble from which people were freed?

Jesus also sympathized with people who were hungry and tired. Again, many readers will know the stories of how in some mysterious way he fed crowds of four thousand and five thousand people at once. Some had tramped many miles to see him and had run short of food while far from home. He did not want them on their return journey to 'faint by the way'.

Some people complained because Jesus went to parties, and not parties given by the most respectable people either. Tax-collectors, who were known as a dishonest crowd, asked him to their feasts. So did others whom people labelled 'sinners'. Jesus laughed at the grumblers. He said that when John the Baptist ate and drank very little, people said he was crazy. When he himself ate and drank like the rest, these people said, 'Look, what a greedy fellow—given to drink too—and a friend of tax-collectors and bad characters'. Readers may find his words in Luke vii. 33, 34. Some whom so-called respectable people despised wanted him to come to their homes. They needed him. So he went.

Probably Jesus felt extra sympathy for the bad characters because he knew that they were not satisfied with themselves. They wanted to be better people. Jesus did not only want people to be healthy and happy, he wanted most of all that they should be good. He knew (and most of us know, if we think honestly about it) that it is the nastiness and weakness in people which cause more suffering than anything else in the world.

People who are not bad characters may be unsatisfied with themselves too, and Jesus had sympathy with

I believe . . . in Jesus Christ [God's] only Son our Lord,

Who was conceived by the Holy Ghost,

Born of the Virgin Mary,

Suffered under Pontius Pilate,

Was crucified, dead and buried:

He descended into hell; the third day he arose again from the dead;

He ascended into heaven,

And sitteth at the right hand of God the Father Almighty;

From thence he shall come to judge the quick and the dead.

them as well. There is the story of the young man who came to him, sure that he had led a good life and yet not satisfied. Everything seemed all right for the moment, but where would it lead? He wanted, he said, 'eternal life'. Jesus said, 'If you want to enter into life, keep the commandments'. The young man was sure that he always had kept them. Still there was something missing. Jesus looked at him very kindly, but he knew where his weak point lay. He said to the young man, 'You are still lacking in one thing. Go home and sell everything that belongs to you. Give the money to the poor. Your wealth will be in heaven. Then come back and follow me.' The young man's face fell. He turned and went sadly away.

This man wanted to be good, yes, but prosperous and comfortable and safe too. So he was 'in Satan's power' without knowing it. To follow Jesus, he must have seen, was to suffer. It meant being surrounded for days on end by crowds of grubby people, sometimes by sick people with horrible diseases: sore eyes, withered arms and legs, even leprosy. Contact with people like that, according to Jewish law, made a man 'unclean'. After touching even one of these people the young man would not be happy till he had washed ceremonially, and he certainly would not feel it right to touch food. Then, at night, he was used to a comfortable mattress in a room where a lamp was always burning. With Jesus he might spend nights in all sorts of places, even on the open ground. Jesus said to another man, 'Foxes have holes, and birds of the air have nests; but the Son of man hath not where to lay his head'. The 'good' young man could not follow so far.

This young man, readers may say, was clearly of the

'soft' kind. Jesus was only asking him to accept the sort of hardship which comes to quite a number of people who are adventurous and keen on doing something worth-while. That is true. If Jesus had only to stand this kind of suffering himself, he might be counted simply as a hardy kind of man, who cared for all sorts of people and had a wonderful gift of healing. He faced worse suffering when he stood up to powerful men who were perfectly satisfied with themselves. They had no idea that they were 'in Satan's power' and that they were leading people astray. What is more, they had no intention of knowing it. To know the truth about themselves could be much too inconvenient.

Who were these powerful men? Readers of *Servants of God at Work* may remember that one group were the Pharisees. They were particularly strict Jews. They believed themselves to be good because they kept all the rules of the Jewish religion carefully. If a Pharisee did break a rule of his religion, he believed that he could make himself right with God by offering a suitable sacrifice. So he kept his slate clean, as it were.

Jesus believed differently. He said that it was not the outside signs of religion that mattered most. The question was, What was the person like inside himself? That, Jesus said, was what matters to God. As any reader can see, you could keep all the rules of your home and school, and go to church regularly, yet be inside a mean, disagreeable person.

With the Pharisees were the Scribes. These men recorded in writing the words of men who claimed to be rabbis or teachers. Much of the teaching was about how the laws of God in the Old Testament should be kept. Jesus often disagreed with the rabbis. God's laws, he said, were made to help people, but the Scribes and Pharisees made them into burdens.

One subject on which, readers may remember, Jesus disagreed with the rabbis was the keeping of the Sabbath. Jesus, of course, believed that the Sabbath should be God's special day. People should rest from work and let their servants and animals rest too. The Scribes had collected long lists of things which people might not do on that day because they were 'work'. For example, all food must be prepared ahead, so no-one might remove husks from grains of corn, even by throwing the grains in the air. Yet Jesus allowed his hungry disciples one Sabbath to pluck ears of corn as they went through a cornfield, and to rub them in their hands to free the grain from the husks. Later, in the synagogue itself, he healed a man with a paralysed hand. When the Pharisees accused him of breaking the Sabbath, he pointed out that their rules allowed them to pull a fallen sheep out of a pit on the Sabbath. Was not a man more important than a sheep? It was lawful, he said, to do a good thing on the Sabbath. Then, says St. Matthew's Gospel, 'the Pharisees went out and held a council how they might destroy him'. How dare he speak as if he knew better than they?

Another group of powerful people who watched Jesus were the chief priests. They knew that wherever he went crowds came to hear him. They knew that many people began to think of him as a prophet. Some were calling him the Messiah. The priests would be glad of an excuse to get rid of this disturbing, uppish fellow.

Jesus knew that the clouds were gathering. In the third year after he began his work, he planned to go up to Jerusalem for the Passover.

Then he took unto him the twelve, and said unto them, Behold, we go up to Jerusalem, and all things that were written by the prophets concerning the Son of man shall be accomplished. For he shall be delivered unto the Gentiles, and shall be mocked and spitefully entreated and spitted on: and they shall scourge him and put him to death: and the third day he shall rise again.

Jesus believed that those people were right who said that he was the Christ. But he was not the kind of Christ that they hoped for, the successful leader who would help them to overcome their Roman masters. He knew how his people had ill-treated prophets who told them the truth. He knew how the second Isaiah (see *Servants of God at Work*) had said that the Messiah would be the Servant of his people, who would suffer for their sakes. It was his duty to tell God's people the truth about God and themselves. He had to do this in the most dangerous place of all, in the Temple, and before the most dangerous people, the chief priests—even if he died for it. And he would die for it.

But Jesus' disciples could not make out what he was talking about.

(*b*) 'SUFFERED UNDER PONTIUS PILATE, WAS CRUCIFIED'

Five days before the Passover lambs were killed, on the day which we call Palm Sunday, Jesus did an unusual thing. He allowed an eager crowd to cheer him and throw palm branches before him as he rode on a donkey into Jerusalem. It was a sign, quietly made, that he claimed to be the Messiah. Five days later another crowd, egged on by the chief priests and elders of the people, were yelling 'Crucify him'. Were many

Latin cross

Latin cross with second transom (to represent the plank on which the accusation was written)

St. Andrew's cross: probably representing first letter of Greek word Xristos (Latin, Christus)

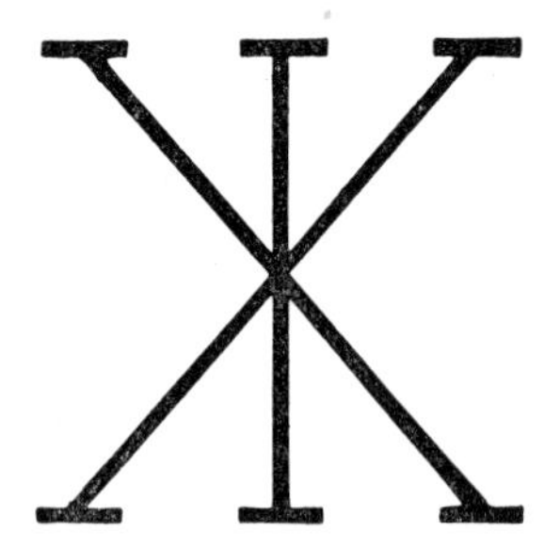

Monogram: representing first letters of names Iesus Ch(X)ristus

of the same people in both crowds? No one knows. Perhaps most of the people in the first crowd were coming in from Galilee. Probably most of those in the second crowd lived in Jerusalem and were ready to back the priests against an outsider. (Jesus was thought of as a Nazarene—a man from Nazareth in Galilee.)

During the four days which lay between, Jesus walked quietly each night to a village outside Jerusalem. By day, with his disciples, he went openly into the great Temple courts. One thing he did which was maddening to those in charge of the Temple. He showed his anger with the men who were busy selling animals for sacrifice in the Temple courts and others who changed the pilgrim's money into special Temple cash. Jesus deliberately overturned their tables and benches. He knew that these people had no right to be in God's house. Their business was a racket, and the priests made money out of it. Jesus also held discussions with the chief priests and the Pharisees. He showed them clearly, especially by parables, that they were unfaithful to God. All these things made the priests more determined than ever to get rid of Jesus, but they dared not take him while the crowds who admired him were about.

In the end, as all the world knows, Jesus was betrayed by Judas, one of his own apostles. Judas knew that on the night before the Passover, Thursday night, Jesus would return to the garden of Gethsemane just outside the city. He could be arrested quietly there. No-one will ever know all Judas' reasons. Whatever they were, he could not resist making a deal of it. He sold his master for thirty pieces of silver. Afterwards he tried to hand the money back, but it was too late.

Not one of the apostles, not even Peter, who had been

so sure that Jesus was the Christ, stood by him in the end. They were all too scared, scared of their own rulers, scared of the Roman government.

The Jews were not allowed by the Romans to order the death penalty. So the priests, having questioned Jesus all night, hurried him in the early morning before the Roman governor. It was easy to accuse him of treason. He said he was Christ, a king. That was treason, they said, against the Emperor, Caesar.

Pontius Pilate the Roman governor would have let Jesus off. He knew that the Jewish leaders wanted to get rid of this remarkable man because they were jealous of him. Pilate made certain from Jesus himself that the kingdom of which he spoke was not of this world. But the Jewish leaders knew the governor's weak spot. 'If you let this man off', they cried, 'you are not Caesar's friend.'

Pilate was afraid that to free Jesus might damage his reputation and that he might lose his post. Rather than let this happen he would allow Jesus to suffer. The chief priests and elders were working up the mob. They were yelling 'Crucify him'. Pilate gave way. He publicly washed his hands before the crowd to show that the fault was not his. 'I am innocent of the blood of this just person. You see to it.' That is what he said. But the result was the same. Everyone had let Jesus down, and he was led away to be crucified.

The Jewish leaders rejoiced. 'He saved others,' they said, 'he can't save himself. If he is the king of Israel, let him come down from the cross and we will believe him.'

Jesus did not come into the world to do things for his own benefit. He came, you remember, to be the bridge between God, the perfect, and sinful men. From the cross he was still able to say to God, 'Father, forgive them, for they know not what they do'.

The night before he died, Jesus had held a supper party for his apostles, a solemn one, a preparation for the Passover. At that supper he had shown the apostles that he knew they would desert him when his enemies came. He knew too that Judas was going, deliberately, to betray him. But he offered bread and wine to all and something special from the dish to the traitor Judas. He showed that however feeble, however bad, the people who called themselves his disciples might be, he still cared for them. That is the way, he showed them, that God cares for us.

That 'last supper' was not forgotten by the apostles. Then, they remembered, Jesus spoke of the bread and wine which they shared as his body and his blood—his life, offered for men. When he broke the thin biscuit-like cake of unleavened bread and handed a portion to each, he said, 'This do in remembrance of me'. In future, Christ's followers were to meet together at appointed times for the 'breaking of bread', as early Christians said. They shared holy bread in the service of Holy Communion.

When Jesus blessed the cup of wine from which all would drink, he spoke of it as standing for a new covenant. As readers know, the apostles had learned when they were boys how in the days of Moses God made a covenant with their forefathers. If they would keep his laws, then God would be their God. What was this new covenant? Jesus said that it was made in his blood—by the giving of his life. Again the apostles could understand, after a fashion, what Jesus meant. They knew that when a covenant was made, the life of an animal was sacrificed to make a bridge between the lives of those concerned. (Look back to page 49 for a reminder about this.) Jesus, they began to understand, was offering his life to link them in a new way with God. Under the old covenant their people had tried to keep the link between themselves and a righteous God by being righteous. Under this new covenant Jesus' disciples would be linked with God by accepting his love for them, which Jesus made them understand.

This is a mystery. But in the service of Holy Communion the cup of wine which is blessed is a symbol of the new covenant, of Christ's life given for love of men.

So day by day, week by week, Christians are reminded that, though Christ suffered on that first Good Friday because men made him suffer, he offered himself willingly for our sakes. His disciples may let him down, but he will not let them down. Christians see in Jesus Christ the Mediator, the bridge between themselves with all their faults and the love of God. This helps to explain why they sing that Jesus came into the world,

> To save us all from Satan's power
> When we were gone astray;
> O tidings of comfort and joy!

—and why that quiet day, Good Friday, is so important.

CHAPTER VIII

The Resurrection

For study

Paradise

Luke xxiii. 43

Jesus' teaching on his resurrection

Mark viii. 31-33

The resurrection story

Mark xvi. 1-7

The disciples cannot believe

Luke xxiv, especially 10-16, 25-37

The Ascension

Luke xxv. 50-52

For extra reading

Thomas cannot believe

John xx. 24-27

St. Paul on the resurrection

1 Corinthians xv. 3-8, 17-22

The third day Christ rose again from the dead

How could he do that? And where had he been in the meantime?

To take the latter question first: the Creed says, 'He descended into hell'. This does not mean that Jesus went to a place where people suffer for their sins. The word Sheol, or hell, was used as one name for that place (or state) in which departed spirits, both good and bad, await the judgement day. There is a Jewish belief, though, that the souls of good men even while waiting for that day are comforted after the troubles of this life. It is almost as though they are in a special part of Sheol, which may be called Paradise. Look at Luke xxiii. 43. You will see that Paradise was the name used by Jesus when speaking to the thief who was dying beside him.

How could Christ possibly rise from the dead? That was a question which, the Gospels show, troubled the minds of his disciples when they first heard the news. Jesus' followers were ordinary, sane people. They knew that he was dead. They knew that a man who respected him had obtained leave from Pilate to carry his body to the grave. Mary Magdalene and other women of their company had observed where it was laid. They had seen a heavy stone rolled in front of the rock tomb. All this had happened before dusk on that Friday (Sabbath Eve) when Jesus died.

Read the verses set from Luke xxiv. You will see that there is no pretence that the disciples believed that the saying of Jesus that he would rise again on the third day had any meaning at all. Women of the company were occupied in their minds as to how they could give proper honour to his dead body. It should have been anointed with fragrant oils, but at the time of that hasty burial, they saw, this had not been done. Several of them—Mary Magdalene was one—determined that as soon as the Sabbath was past they would somehow manage to carry out this anointing. It was the last thing they could do for their friend. Only, who would open the tomb for them?

Not the men among the disciples. They seem to have gathered together miserably in some private place. They had had such faith in Jesus. They had been sure that he was the Messiah. They had expected to play important parts in helping him to bring in a new kingdom. Then he had been seized and executed as if he was a common criminal. None of them had even had the courage to stand by him. Now he was dead. The Jewish leaders would have their eye on them next. This was the end.

These men had done what many people do today—chosen which bits of Jesus' teaching they would believe, and left the rest.

The 'third day', Sunday morning, came. The women hurried out before dawn. They found the tomb open and the body of Jesus gone. Then they were amazed by a vision of an angel, who made clear to them that Jesus Christ was risen.

This is told in St. Mark's Gospel, which gives the earliest account which we have of what took place. The stories about that day were handed on by word of mouth and written down later at different times. The

From a church cross
Jesus Christ: sacrifice; priest; king

other three Gospels tell the same story, but, as most readers will know, the details are not all the same.

The women, when they had got over their agitation, told the men. The men took the news as might any men today: they did not believe a word of it. Look at the way St. Luke expresses this in Luke xxiv. 11. But that was, of course, not for any of them the end of the story. Many of the readers of this book will already know some at least of the events which followed Christ's resurrection—how he appeared to Mary Magdalene in the garden, to two men on a walk, to Peter and John and two other disciples when they were fishing, and to 'the Twelve'. When St. Paul wrote a letter to Christians in Corinth about twenty years afterwards, he said that Jesus also appeared to 'more than five hundred brethren at one time, most of whom still survive, though some have fallen asleep'.

That Jesus whom they knew and loved rose from the dead made all the difference to his first followers, though some took a lot of convincing that he really was alive. Belief in his resurrection has made all the difference in the world to Christians up to this very day. At Easter we sing:

> The three sad days have quickly sped;
> He rises glorious from the dead;
> All glory to our risen Head,
> Alleluia.

Of course the Resurrection was a miracle of God—outside the ordinary ways in which his laws of nature work. But why should it not be out of the ordinary? Jesus was not an ordinary person. St. Paul spoke of him once as God's 'firstfruits'—the first of those who have 'fallen asleep' to rise from the dead. Paul said that if Christ did not rise from the dead, then we should have no proof of an after-life at all. There would be no proof, as it were, that Christ by dying for our sins has broken the chains that tie us to earth and has made us free of God's company. But, Paul said:

> No, Christ has risen from the dead, the firstfruits of all those who have fallen asleep.

(This is a modern version of words in 1 Corinthians xv.) Like Adam, all men are mortal: their bodies die. With Christ their spirits come alive.

It is this belief, that Christ not only died for them but rose again, that makes Christians able to sing at Easter:

> Lord, by the stripes which wounded thee,
> From death's dread sting thy servants free,
> That we may live, and sing to thee
> Alleluia.

Forty days after Easter comes Ascension Day. This is always on a Thursday, as readers can calculate for themselves, and is not a public holiday. Some schools make it a whole holiday. Children from certain other schools attend a special service on that day. On Ascension Day Christians remember how Jesus Christ spoke some last words to the apostles and then, as it seemed, 'was parted from them and carried up into heaven'.

No-one can explain how this thing happened. Nor does that matter. Jesus came from God: he went to God. But he told the disciples first that they would not be left alone.

CHAPTER IX

Jesus Christ our judge

For study

The rich man and Lazarus
Luke xvi. 19-31

The sheep and the goats
Matthew xxv. 31-46

Herein is love
1 John iv. 9-11

The return of the Lord
Luke xii. 35-38

For extra reading

The bridegroom comes
Matthew xxv. 1-13

Jesus sits at the right hand of God the Father Almighty, from whence he shall come to judge the quick [living] and the dead

We think in pictures and talk in pictures. The Jews used to see the sky as a dome. There were windows in it, through which God sent rain when he wished. Above the dome was heaven. God was enthroned in heaven. Early Christians might picture Jesus, who had triumphed over sin and death, sitting at the right hand of the throne of God.

We know that the sky is not a dome and that God does not sit upon a solid throne or even upon clouds. But we still have to make our own pictures when we think of God the Father, the ruler of the universe, and Jesus Christ whom we know as the Son of God.

Again, the Jewish people pictured the judgement day as a fixed day at the end of history, when God would sit as judge of the people of the world. The good would be saved and the wicked be cast into a place called Gehenna, which was under the world. We cannot imagine one single day when God will act as a judge to all the many, many millions of the world. What pictures should we have in mind when we think of Jesus as our judge? Can we find anything in his teaching to help us?

Jesus, of course, used pictures himself, all the time. The symbols which he used were ones to which the people of his time were specially accustomed, but they are not too difficult for us to understand.

Three parables are set *For study* which show something

of Jesus' teaching about judgement. One is the parable of the rich man and Lazarus. This may have been a parable which Jesus learned as a boy, not one which he invented. It is about two men. One was a self-centred person, who happened to have everything he wanted. The other was a poor sick beggar, Lazarus, who would have been grateful for any help he could get.

The rich man before his death was probably confident that all was well with him. Most likely he was a Sadducee. These people, as readers of *Servants of God at Work* may remember, did not believe in an after-life. If this life was all, why not fill it with as much pleasure as you could? It is possible, though, that he may have been the kind of man who was quite sure that he said the right prayers and made the right sacrifices, so was a 'good' Jew. Lazarus the beggar had no chance either to enjoy himself or to offer sacrifices. The tough village dogs knew, however, that he was someone they should treat gently.

Both the rich man and Lazarus died and went to Sheol, or hell, to await the final judgement. The rich man found himself in misery. Lazarus, on the other hand, was in Abraham's bosom, a quaint way of saying that he was treated as a 'good' Jew. He received there the comforting care that no-one had troubled to give him on earth. It was the man who had failed in love for his poor neighbour who had become the outsider.

Now read this parable in Luke xvi for yourself.

Have you noticed that suffering brought out something good in the once selfish man? He became humble enough to ask for a little comfort from the dirty beggar whom he had once shunned. He began to think of his brothers. He was certain that they were as self-satisfied as he. Could not Lazarus be allowed to carry a warning to them? Have you noticed, too, that this was not allowed? Each man was responsible for making proper use of the Bible teaching that he must have had in school and synagogue. The brother in Sheol had to endure the misery of knowing that no miracle would save the others from following the way he had come.

In Matthew xxv are three parables of Jesus which we might call parables of the judgement day itself. But in none of them is God or Jesus pictured as a judge. In the first we see a bridegroom coming to claim his bride on the wedding night. In the second is a master returning from a long journey (see page 202). In the third is a glorious shepherd king at the rounding up of his flocks.

Before you go further, read the third parable, in Matthew xxv. 31-46.

Do you see one special likeness between the parable and the story of the rich man and Lazarus? In both these parables, people get surprises, pleasant or unpleasant. They are not judged according to their own view of themselves. The question is, Have they failed in love to God, shown in love to their neighbour?

So this coming of God in judgement on his people has something to do with love. This seems mysterious, but the first Christians were sure of it. The person whom they expected to see was the Jesus whom they knew. St. Luke explains at the opening of the book of the Acts of the Apostles that when Jesus was taken up into heaven his apostles received the promise:

> This same Jesus, which is taken up from you into heaven, shall so come in like manner as ye have seen him go into heaven.

'This same Jesus' loved them and gave his life for them. All their lives they hoped that he would suddenly return in a way that they could see. Meanwhile they went on working for him.

We have not seen Jesus the man, as his apostles saw him. We must find him in the Gospels. But even with their help, to 'love God' or 'love Jesus'—sometimes the idea seems quite impossible to get at. Are we to be judged for not loving God when it seems quite an impossible thing to do?

One way is to remember that God has done the loving first, as a mother loves a baby before the baby has any idea what loving means. An early Christian wrote:

> Herein is love, not that we loved God, but that he loved us, and sent his Son to be [an atonement] for our sins.

A second thing to remember is—what our parables make clear—that God often judges our love to him by our attitude to other people.

Our attitude to other people: it is that which shows us up. The writer of this book once, when on jury service, saw a group of youths standing in the dock. They looked well-dressed and well-fed. They lived in a pleasant town where there was no unemployment. They could earn quite enough money for their needs and pleasures. Yet all were accused of breaking-in and taking other people's goods. Next it appeared that three of them had applied for legal assistance. Each wished a barrister from the court to come forward and make the best case for him that he could. The judge asked each lad who would provide the barrister's fee. Each one replied, 'My mother, sir'. 'Oh,' said the judge '—your mother.' These youths were accused of breaking-in and robbing; they had brought disgrace on the mothers who cared for them. By taking money from their mothers at such a time they made their selfishness show up even more clearly.

Most of us keep within the law, but we may be pretty selfish too. Suppose a boy (or girl) has a good mother whom he (or she) believes that he loves and respects. A message comes early one morning during the holidays: 'Grandmother is ill: will mother please come at once?' The mother says, 'I must leave you in charge. I can't stay even to do the washing-up or make the beds. Keep an eye on Johnnie. Do the best that you can, and don't forget to run to the baker before closing time.' Then she is gone.

Now this son thinks that he loves his mother—if he thinks of it at all. What is he going to do in her absence? Is he going to say, 'There is plenty of time to get the work done', and lounge through the morning? Is he going to get caught up with friends in the afternoon? Finally, when his mother returns, will he be found still down the road, or frantically trying to straighten things up while Johnnie skirmishes round trying to borrow a loaf? Or is he going to put the house to rights before he does anything else? Is he going to keep a firm eye on Johnnie? Will the kettle be filled and the table be ready for a meal when his mother returns?

The writer has deliberately used 'he' throughout this last paragraph, though boys may not like it. (Some fancy that giving a hand in the house is not a man's work.) Will girls, please, go back and read 'she' for 'he' throughout the paragraph.

The mother, back in her home, is bound to judge her

child by what she sees. Her judgement will be the judgement of love. She will not expect things to be done as well as she could do them herself. But if the son (or the daughter) has proved selfish and untrustworthy, a mother cannot think very highly of his (or her) love for her. Love shows itself in faithfulness.

Suppose the boy (or the girl) is the 'slick' kind, who can fake at the last minute an appearance of things being all right. Suppose Johnnie has scrambled through the day safely and does not 'talk'. The mother may be deceived, pleased to find what seems to be a welcome—perhaps it is a welcome. But judgement is there all the time—the judgement of God, the judgement of Jesus. Our conscience shows us that.

Jesus spoke no parable that we know of which described the home-coming of a mother. He did speak, though, of the coming of a bridegroom to claim his bride. (The parable is set *For extra reading.*) Of the bride's maidens, half were not ready. Their lamps were without oil. They could not light the bridegroom into the marriage feast. In the end they found themselves shut out.

These maidens were unfaithful. Another parable (in Luke xii. 35-38) tells of faithful servants. Their master has been to a wedding. This again, in eastern fashion, is at night. The tired servants do not wrap themselves in their heavy coats and lie down to sleep. They stay awake, even into the third watch (after 2 o'clock in the morning). They keep their lamps trimmed and torches at hand. When they hear knocking on the outer courtyard gate they know that their lord has come home. Such servants will not go supperless to bed. The lord will serve them himself.

The end of this parable may surprise us. (It would surprise eastern hearers more. Whoever heard of such a thing—a master waiting on his servants? They were for his use day and night, weren't they?) But the parable shows that we may expect from Jesus, if he is our master, the surprising treatment that love gives to love, that faithfulness gives to faithfulness. He may return to us at an unexpected moment of our lives, in the hour of our death, at some time in history known only to God, or when history ends. Meanwhile there are some lines from the *Te Deum* (see *Servants of God at Work*) which can be a prayer for us all:

We believe that thou shalt come to be our judge.
We therefore pray thee help thy servants,
Whom thou hast redeemed with thy precious blood.
Make them to bc numbered with thy saints
In glory everlasting.

CHAPTER X

Whitsuntide and Trinity

For study

Jesus explains Isaiah
Luke iv. 14-22

Whit Sunday
Acts ii. 1-8

New power and courage
Acts iii. 11; iv. 1-10, 15-20

Teaching on the Holy Spirit
John xiv. 15-17, 26

The blessing of the Trinity
2 Corinthians xiii. 14

For extra reading

Advice from a prisoner—St. Paul
Galatians v. 16-25

I believe in the Holy Ghost

JESUS has ascended. Jesus will return in judgement. In the meantime his promise stands that his followers will not be left without help. God will send to them the Holy Spirit.

The special day given to the honour of the Holy Spirit is Whit Sunday. 'Whit' is probably an ancient spelling of 'white', so we might call this Sunday, White Sunday. In the northern part of Europe it was once a custom that baptisms should take place on this Sunday. The people baptized wore white clothes. White Sunday would be thought of as baptism Sunday. (In warmer lands, farther south, baptisms were usually at Easter.)

On Whit Sunday many people hear words from the second chapter of the Acts of the Apostles read in church. Readers probably know already the story told there, of how on the Jewish feast of Pentecost the Spirit of God came like tongues of fire upon the waiting followers of Christ. They were so filled with this Spirit that they were able to make the teaching of Jesus clear to people who spoke many different languages.

To the apostles it must have seemed marvellous that God should strengthen them, of all people, with his Spirit, to speak out boldly. Of course they knew that in past times prophets had been filled with God's Spirit. In school and on the Sabbath they must have heard the words of Isaiah of Babylon:

The Spirit of the Lord God is upon me; because the Lord hath anointed me to preach good tidings unto the meek; he hath sent me to bind up the broken-hearted, to proclaim liberty to the captives, and the opening of the prison to them that are bound; to proclaim the acceptable year of the Lord.

Jesus, the apostles knew, was filled with the Spirit of the Lord. Some of them were probably there one Sabbath, in the synagogue at Nazareth, soon after Jesus began to teach throughout Galilee. As an honoured visitor to his home town, he was asked to read the passage for the day from one of the books of the prophets. He chose a passage from Isaiah lxi, of which St. Luke's version is set *For study*—a short passage which gave a text for a sermon. He began his sermon by saying that all that the prophet had said applied to himself. The congregation listened intently for a time, then found that Jesus was telling them home-truths. Furious, they tried to lynch him on the spot.

The apostles, though, had trusted Jesus. When he asked them to join his band they had done so. They had found that what he said was true; the Spirit of the Lord was upon him, he did bring a message of cheer to troubled people. He was, in fact, the Christ.

But what about themselves? The apostles were ordinary people. While Jesus was alive they had only half-understood what he taught. When danger came they ran away. They found it difficult to get into their heads that their master really had risen from the dead. Now they were sure. They knew that they must hand on the good news. But how? Jesus had promised them help from God if they waited. So they did wait, joining in the Temple services and meetings for prayer with others who believed. On that first Whit Sunday, the order to speak to the world came to them, and they found themselves able to obey.

I believe in the Holy Ghost;
The holy Catholic Church;
The Communion of Saints;
The Forgiveness of sins;
The Resurrection of the body;
And the life everlasting.

That happened long ago. It was a kind of starting-off day for Christian missionaries. Such an exciting sense of the power of God's Spirit cannot often be known. When we sing:

> Come, Holy Ghost, our souls inspire,
> And lighten with celestial fire,

we do not expect to see outward signs of fire. The thing that matters is to know that the Holy Spirit was not a gift sent only into the first little Church just for a few minutes and then snatched away. He has been there in the Christian Church ever since. Jesus Christ called himself the vine, his followers the branches. The Holy Spirit might be said to be like the sap in the vine. He can help each branch to produce good grapes.

A prayer used at christenings asks God that he will give his Holy Spirit to the person baptized, that he or she may be born again and made an heir of everlasting salvation. Whenever you see a group of Christians really 'alive', minding how they serve God and their fellow men, you can be sure that the promised Helper is among them.

Peter and John quickly showed in their lives the difference that the presence of the Holy Spirit can make. Readers may remember how some time after the first Whit Sunday they were seized by the Temple police and brought before the people whom they most feared, the rulers of the Jews. There was no question any longer of trying to run away. Before the high priest, they openly said that it was through Christ's name that they had healed a lame man. Moreover, they refused to be silent about Jesus: 'For', they said, 'we cannot but speak the things which we have seen and heard'.

These apostles found that the Holy Spirit gave them what we call moral courage—power to stand up for what you are sure is true, however frightening the circumstances. This fitted with the teaching which Jesus gave them, and which it took them all their time really to understand. Look at John xiv. 15-17. Here is a modern version of the passage (the speaker is Jesus):

> If you love me you will keep my commands, and I will ask the Father to give you another Helper to be with you for ever, even the Spirit of truth: the world cannot receive him, because it neither sees nor knows him, but you know him, because he remains with you and will be within you.

To ourselves today, Jesus might say, 'If you are on my side, you will try to obey my teaching. This is difficult for you alone. You need help to understand what is right. You need help to do right. If you ask God for my sake to send you that help, he will do so.'

Look at the prayer printed on page 48 (readers who have a Prayer Book will find it is the Collect for the Ninth Sunday after Trinity). This prayer asks God, in a short way, to send his Spirit to the help of our spirits, so that we may think and do right things.

The teaching of Jesus from St. John's Gospel which was quoted above is part of a 'discourse', a talk or explanation, which the writer says Jesus gave to his closest friends. It comes at the end of the story of the Last Supper. St. John's Gospel was not written for many years after Jesus' crucifixion. As the writer thought over Jesus teaching, he may have added to that after-supper talk things that belonged to other evenings. In this 'discourse' Jesus explains to his apostles the one-ness of God the Father, himself the

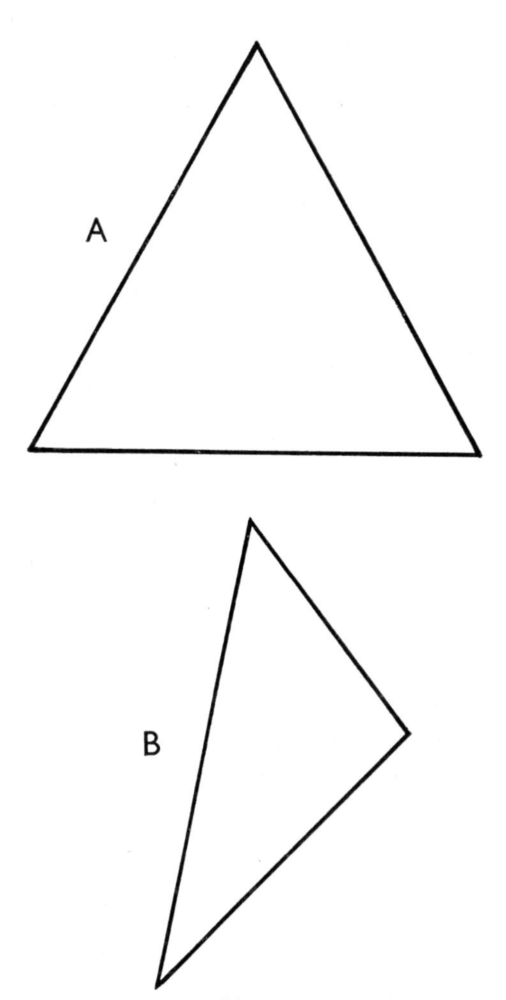

Triangles

Son, and the Comforter (or Helper), the Holy Spirit whom the Father will send in his name. We can learn from the discourse, with time and thought, the meaning of the Trinity.

Readers may say, 'We believe in one God. How can he at the same time be three?' Look back to page 89 (*A*). You see a triangle. Only one triangle. But it is made of three lines, three parts, and if any one of these was missing, it would not be a triangle at all. All three are necessary to make one whole. In this triangle each side, and so each angle, is equal. So, when we speak of God as Trinity, we say that each person, Father, Son, and Holy Spirit, matters to us in making God real to us. Each is an 'aspect', a part of our picture, of the one God.

Illustration *B* is another triangle. Here the sides are of different lengths and so the angles are different. But you still cannot say that one side or angle matters less than the others. You still need each to make up your triangle. So we say, God in heaven; Jesus Christ on earth; the Spirit, able to help us in our innermost thoughts and feelings: all seem different from each other, but all are 'aspects' of the one God.

This is, of course, a flat explanation of a mystery. Some readers may find a word picture easier. Suppose there is a young child who has a kind father. The child knows him as the person who plays with him in the garden, brings home sweets, and takes him to the pantomime. Then he discovers that outside people consider his daddy a most alarming person, for he is a judge, with power to sentence people to imprisonment or even death. Then the child's father takes him for a continental holiday, and suddenly he appears as another person, a man who seems at home while exchanging all kinds of jokes with foreign people in their own language—a 'citizen of Europe'. The child has discovered three sides of one person—all real, all different. Readers can think out other pictures of this kind from among their own friends.

The one God may show different sides of himself to us in different ways.

It is not surprising that after Whit Sunday comes Trinity Sunday. No public holiday is connected with this Sunday. Readers who belong to Oxford may know that the summer term at Oxford University is known as the Trinity term. Those readers who have Prayer Books can see that the Sundays labelled Sundays after Trinity last, not only through the summer term, but through the summer holidays as well, and right on to the time when we begin to think about Christmas. On Trinity Sunday and those other Sundays people sing the hymn which begins:

> Holy, holy, holy! Lord God Almighty!
> Early in the morning our song shall rise to thee;
> Holy, holy, holy! Merciful and mighty!
> God in three Persons, blessèd Trinity!

CHAPTER XI

Where we come in

For study

Members of one body

Romans xii. 4, 5

Romans xiv. 7-9

St. Paul on sin, sinners, and eternal life

Romans iii. 23

Romans iv. 8

Romans vi. 9-12, 22-23

How are the dead raised up?

1 Corinthians xv. 35-38, 42-44, 49

The holy city

Revelation xxi. 10-11, 22-27

Revelation xxii. 4, 5

The prayer on page 98, another version

Ephesians iii. 14-21

For extra reading

Jesus' teaching on the resurrection

Matthew xxii. 23-32

I believe in the holy Catholic Church, the Communion of Saints, the Forgiveness of sins, the Resurrection of the body, and the life everlasting

HERE are five things which Christians believe, that have specially to do with themselves.

Six verses of a well-known hymn are printed over the page. (Readers can find in hymn-books two other verses which have been left out.) Look at the verses here and see, if you can, how many of the five Christian beliefs stated above show themselves.

I believe in the holy Catholic Church. Perhaps no reader can find where that belief shows up, but it is there. Catholic, as readers of *Servants of God at Work* know, means universal. The Catholic Church is made up of all those who have been baptized in the name of the Lord Jesus Christ. But how 'holy'? If that means something like 'very good', no-one can say that all baptized people are, or have been, very good. In fact, 'holy' does not mean quite that. It means set apart for the service of God. People who join the armed forces are set apart for the service of their king, or queen, and their country. Christians are set apart as servants and soldiers of God and his Church. When we sing in verse 2 of Christ's soldiers 'faithful, true and bold', we are singing of members of his Church who are still on earth. We want them to show as good a spirit as the saints, those other members of the Church, showed in their time. So this verse might be called a prayer for the holy Catholic Church.

I believe in the Communion of Saints. Every verse is about saints. Only verse 3 speaks of 'communion'.

Who are the saints about whom we sing? The answer is that you can think of saints in two ways. First, there is a long list of named people, canonized saints. Many readers have heard of the Canon of the Old Testament and that of the New Testament. In each case a fixed collection of books goes to make up the Canon. In rather the same way, there is a settled list, a long one, of what we might call 'official' saints. (The apostles and many early martyrs are included in this list. See *Servants of God at Work*, Part Two.) They have been 'canonized'. Their names are in the 'canon' or list of saints. Many saints in the canon give their names to saints' days. When the Church of England separated her government from that of the Roman Catholic Church, she did not, readers will remember, cast aside all the saints' days. But she did cease to take part in adding to the catalogue. The Roman Catholic Church still adds names of certain specially holy people to the canon.

Secondly, when we sing 'For all the saints who from their labours rest', we may not be thinking of these canonized saints. We may think of people we have known and cared for, people whom we believe were true servants of God, though they did nothing wonderful.

'O blest communion.' The word communion often means a talking together of friends, or a sharing. The saints who have left this world still share with us and with each other in being members of Christ's Church. They belong to what we call the Church triumphant. We, if we are 'live' Christians, may be called members

For all the saints who from their labours rest,
Who thee by faith before the world confessed,
Thy name, O Jesu, be for ever blest.

Oh may thy soldiers, faithful, true, and bold,
Fight as the saints who nobly fought of old,
And win, with them, the victor's crown of
gold.

O blest communion, fellowship divine!
We feebly struggle, they in glory shine;
Yet all are one in thee, for all are thine.

The golden evening brightens in the west;
Soon, soon to faithful warriors comes their
rest:
Sweet is the calm of Paradise the blest.

But lo, there breaks a yet more glorious day;
The saints triumphant rise in bright array:
The King of Glory passes on his way.

From earth's wide bounds, from ocean's
farthest coast,
Through gates of pearl streams in the count-
less host,
Singing to Father, Son and Holy Ghost
Alleluia!

of the Church militant, that is the Church still on earth, fighting for the right. Some people choose the anniversary of the death of a Christian friend to go specially to the service of Holy Communion. In that service Christians are reminded that, whether they can see each other or not, they share together the new life offered by Jesus Christ, who died for us all and rose again.

I believe in the Forgiveness of sins. Readers will not find that directly in the verses. Perhaps, 'We feebly struggle, they in glory shine' is the nearest to it. We know that none of us, not even the greatest saints, have been perfect soldiers. 'All have sinned and come short of the glory of God': that is what St. Paul said. But Jesus Christ has shown that God is waiting to accept each honest apology. The saints, when they fell in the fight, with God's help picked themselves up and fought on. We can do the same.

I believe in the Resurrection of the body. Probably every reader will suggest the second line of the fifth verse as fitting that. No-one knows what kind of body will be given to Christ's soldiers and saints at the resurrection. When the Sadducees asked Jesus stupid questions about marriage in the next world, he told them sharply that they did not understand the Scriptures or the power of God. 'In the resurrection, they neither marry nor are given in marriage, but are as the angels of God.'

We cannot find out about our own resurrection bodies from the stories of the resurrection of Jesus Christ. When Jesus appeared to his friends, they had in some way to look steadily at him before they knew it was he. Then he seemed altogether the same person as they had known on earth. But Jesus was God as well as man. His body did not 'see corruption'. Ours, because we are ordinary, earthly people, return to dust. That does not mean, however, that God cannot clothe our spirits, each with a body which 'fits' and in which our friends will know us.

Have you ever had a dream like this? You see someone who is dead, or whom you have not seen for a long time. You say, 'I dreamt I saw X last night'. Somebody asks, 'How did he look?' He remembers X, as you do, an old, lame man. You say, 'Well, when I come to think about it, he didn't look like X. He looked younger, and he whizzed past me on a motor bike, wearing a crash helmet. But it was X all right. I knew his smile.' In your dream, it was the person that you recognized. The outside change in his looks did not seem to matter. In the resurrection, we may know each other, even if we 'look' quite different. One of your readings shows how St. Paul tried to explain the difference between our 'spiritual' bodies and the 'earthly' ones in which we now live.

I believe in the life everlasting. The writer of the hymn does not take his procession of saints farther than the gates of pearl which lead to the holy city. (Look at verse 6.) He is thinking of the city described in the Revelation of St. John the Divine, a city built of gold and jewels, the loveliest things that the writer could imagine. None of us can really know what heaven is like. The thing to remember is that if we want to enter into eternal life, the time to begin is now. As Jesus showed the rich young man (look back to Chapter VII), it is not a matter of waiting till you die. It is a matter of taking action at once. So much depends on how you begin the adventure—and the fight.

To end—an early prayer of the Church. (Stop after each sentence. Do you understand it? If not, look back to the chapter suggested in brackets, or to another which you think may help to refresh your mind.)

I fall on my knees to the Father of our Lord Jesus Christ (III), that Father from whom all fatherhood in heaven and earth takes its title (II). May he, out of the rich treasury of his glory, strengthen you through his spirit with a power that reaches your innermost being (X). May Christ find a dwelling-place, through faith, in your hearts; may your lives be rooted in love, founded on love (VII). May you and all the saints be enabled to measure, in all its breadth and length and height and depth, the love of Christ, to know what passes knowledge (IX and XI). May you be filled with all the completion God has to give (XI). He whose power is at work in us is powerful enough, and more than powerful enough, to carry out his purpose beyond all our hopes and dreams; may he be glorified in the Church, and in Christ Jesus, to the last generation of eternity (XI). Amen.

PART TWO

What are we to do?

by

A. F. Titterton

CHAPTER XII

Beginning at home

For study

Commandments concerned with other people

Matthew xix. 16-19

The way of the wise child

Proverbs i. 7-8

Proverbs vi. 20-22

Proverbs x. 1

Proverbs xiii. 1

It is Corban

Mark vii. 9-13

St. Paul on children and parents

Ephesians vi. 1-4

For extra reading

The use of the stick

Proverbs xiii. 24

Proverbs xix. 18

Parents and children

Proverbs xxiii. 22-25

WHAT am I to do? People ask that question far more often than 'What am I to believe?' In fact, what you are prepared to do depends a great deal of the time on what you really believe. It is when you have strong convictions on a subject that you are most prepared to put yourself out—and sometimes other people too— to get your idea carried through.

Suppose a girl has a strong conviction that she will look a sight at the dance next Saturday night unless she has had a new 'hair-do'. She will go to a great deal of trouble to be sure she has the money, and the appointment for the hairdresser. She will be prepared to take aspirin and go to bed early to get rid of her cold, so that she will not be unfit for the appointment. The same thing is true in what other people may think more important matters.

Do you remember the young man who had an idea that he was not doing all that he could to make the best of his life, and who came to Jesus asking how he could obtain 'eternal life'? Do you remember too that this does not just mean life for ever and ever but life of the best quality, the life open to members of the City of God? Jesus gave that young man a practical answer. He quoted a list from the Commandments. To keep those commandments, that would be a useful beginning, he seemed to suggest. The young man was sure, though, that he was not a beginner. He had kept all these from his youth up, he said. Only then did Jesus suggest something harder, as it seemed, for him to do. He was not ready to try.

The Ten Commandments, including five which the young man was sure he had always kept, can be found in full in Exodus xx. The most important sentences are printed opposite this page. Look at those sentences. Notice that eight out of the ten laws do not tell you what to do but what not to do. Notice again that the first three are concerned specially with how we shall behave towards God. The fourth is concerned with God and (in full) with other people; the last six with behaviour towards others. It was five of this last group, according to the account given in St. Matthew, that Jesus pointed out to the young man. Finally he quoted the 'covering' commandment, 'Thou shalt love thy neighbour as thyself'. Start with everyday life, he seemed to say.

Everyday life begins at home. Here we are faced with the fifth Commandment. This is a commandment which tells us something we must do: 'Honour thy father and thy mother'. In other times and in other lands, young people have had little chance to avoid honouring their parents outwardly. They have been brought up to expect their parents to rule their lives, to choose their work for them, to plan their marriage. Nowadays British boys and girls expect to have a big say both in choosing their jobs and planning their free time; and they certainly expect to be free to choose whom they shall marry.

How then do we show honour to our parents? There are obvious suggestions: (1) by being polite to them, not answering back or 'cheeking' them; (2) by remembering times that matter to them, such as their birthdays. Honouring means more than that though: when you are a child it means doing what they tell you; it means when

The Ten Commandments

FROM EXODUS XX

God says :

I

Thou shalt have no other gods before me. (*v. 3*)

II

Thou shalt not make unto thee any graven image. (*v. 4*)

III

Thou shalt not take the name of the Lord thy God in vain. (*v. 7*)

IV

Remember the Sabbath day to keep it holy. (*v. 8*)

V

Honour thy father and thy mother. (*v. 12*)

VI

Thou shalt not kill. (*v. 13*)

VII

Thou shalt not commit adultery. (*v. 14*)

VIII

Thou shalt not steal. (*v. 15*)

IX

Thou shalt not bear false witness against thy neighbour. (*v. 16*)

X

Thou shalt not covet thy neighbour's house . . . nor anything that is thy neighbour's. (*v. 17*)

you are older that you are ready to listen to their advice. The readings from Proverbs set *For study* speak of this. Honouring means, too, being ready to help them. Jesus showed this when he spoke out to a group of Pharisees about 'Corban'.

At that time public arrangements for supporting old people were not known. There was no State Insurance, no Old Age Pensions. When parents were in need, ill perhaps, or past work, it was expected that their children would give them a helping hand. Some people, Pharisees included, resented this. They did not want to spend time or money helping their parents. The Pharisees had a polite way of showing it. They said, 'It is Corban, the help which I would have given you'. The word Corban meant, in the beginning, a gift or sacrifice to God; but its meaning in time became much more like 'something I have vowed to hold back'. The son who said, 'This money might have been at your service, but it is Corban', was really saying, 'I have vowed not to help you with a penny, however great your need'.

Jesus, as the passage set *For study* in Mark vii shows, attacked the Pharisees' custom of using the pious phrase 'It is Corban' to avoid their duty. He said that it was one of the ways in which they made God's word of no effect. To say 'It is Corban' was, in fact, a way of cancelling out your duty to your parents.

Young people today are not often asked to support their parents; but in most homes there is help that sons and daughters ought to give. Many readers will think at once of the daily chores. None is likely to say, 'The washing-up and the bed-making and the shoe-cleaning and the picking-up-of-my-clothes from the floor, these are Corban'; but it is easy enough to give a 'good' excuse for avoiding these things. 'I mustn't be late for school'—or work, or Bible class, or Scouts, or my dress-making class, or some other 'good' activity. Again it is easy enough to find something else that we 'ought' to do when we are asked on a special occasion to help in a way which we find unpleasant or which makes us feel foolish. (The writer used to object to taking notes and messages to houses where people talked piously or asked personal questions about school or home. Why could not someone else do it?) Yet to give this kind of help, like assisting with chores, is a way of keeping the fifth Commandment.

The boy or girl who has left school to go to work but still lives at home easily uses 'Corban'. There was a young couple, George and Mavis, who did so, though they had no idea of it. George was apprenticed to a skilled trade. Mavis was pretty and smart and did not mind hard work. They were both eager to be married as soon as he had mastered his trade, and they meant to have a good home. So they determined to save all they could. At the same time they wanted to enjoy their engagement. Their homes, unfortunately, were many miles apart, so to avoid missing week-ends together they spent a good deal on long-distance coach fares. Then tickets for week-end dances and football matches cost money. Where could the saving come from? It came because, though both were earning quite good money, neither George nor Mavis paid their parents half of what it cost to keep them at home. Mavis' mother was expected, too, to act as an unpaid laundress. Each week a large bundle of pretty clothes was handed to her for washing and ironing. This young couple's money was vowed towards the cost of the lovely wedding and the

THE

PILGRIM'S PROGRESS,

Under the SIMILITUDE of a

DREAM.

AS I walked through the wilderneſs of this world, I lighted on a certain place, where was a den, and laid me down in that place to ſleep: and as I ſlept, I dreamed a dream. I dreamed, and behold, *I ſaw a man clothed with rags ſtanding in a certain place, with his face from his own houſe, a book in his hand, and a great burden upon his back,* Iſa. lxiv. 6. Luke xvi. 33. Pſalm xxxviii. 4. Heb. ii. 2. Acts xiv. 31. I looked and ſaw him open the book and read therein; and as he read, he wept and trembled; and not being able longer to contain, he brake out with a lamentable cry, ſaying, *What ſhall I do?* Acts ii. 37.

The goal.

The opening of 'Pilgrim's Progress' (*see page 5*)

modern home. It was 'Corban' as far as their parents were concerned.

How did the parents take it? someone may ask. They were kind people, anxious for their children to be happy and they said very little; but the mothers especially, with younger children to care for, got extra tired, extra in need of a good time themselves.

George and Mavis did not mean to be selfish. Both thought that they were very fond of their parents; but when they failed to pull their weight at home, as soon as this got in the way of their own plans, they treated the fifth Commandment lightly.

Sometimes boys and girls as they grow up find it difficult to get on with their parents, or perhaps with one parent. When children are small they take their parents' ways for granted. As they grow older they begin to see the parents from outside, as it were, as human beings with their own faults and weaknesses. Usually this works quite well. The son or daughter begins to make allowances for 'Mum's ways' and 'Dad's fancies', as the parents have made allowance for Tom's or Mary's special ways since they were babies. At times, though, a parent seems—and perhaps is—unkind or unreasonable or misunderstanding. Then it is easy to feel resentful. This is not a new difficulty. The passage set *For study* from St. Paul's letter to the Ephesians shows that the apostle knew that the blame might not be on one side only. St. Paul was sure that children should obey parents: a prosperous nation is built out of orderly homes. He knew, though, that parents may behave in a way which is bound to make the children angry.

What can the children do about it? They certainly cannot start putting their parents to rights. That only makes bad worse. Anyhow the disagreement may not be a question of right or wrong. It may be that the boy or girl and the father or mother just do not fit in with each other. The child can at least do two things: first, keep in mind all that his parents have done or are doing for him (or her); secondly, stick to the rules about politeness and helpfulness. Later on he (or she) may discover that he is getting to understand his parents better.

Boys and girls may belong to families where the parents continuously disagree or have separated. These young people are faced with extra problems. One difficult thing they can try to do: to avoid judging one or other of their parents harshly before they themselves have longer experience of life.

CHAPTER XIII

Thou shalt not steal

For study

Faithfulness and earthly possessions
Luke xvi. 10-13
(mammon = worldly riches)

Advice on lying and stealing
Ephesians iv. 25, 28

Giving, not getting
Luke vi. 30-35
James ii. 14-17

For extra reading

Poor, but a giver
Luke xxi. 1-4

'STEAL a pin, and you'll steal anything.' Jennie's mother had said that plenty of times. Jennie knew what it meant. Never take anything, however small, that isn't yours. Once you begin you don't know how you'll end. Still, Jennie did want a sweet. Her mother's back was turned as she worked at the kitchen table. Jennie reached up quickly and took one sweet out of the jar on the shelf. No one but mother was supposed to touch that jar. Jennie was too small to know that mother had a way of keeping an eye on the antics of her youngest with the help of the kitchen looking-glass.

Dinner-time came. Brothers and sisters clattered in from school. After the meal, down came the jar. One sweet all round, that was the rule. 'No sweet for you, Jennie,' said her mother, 'you stole one earlier.' Jennie was horrified. 'No, I didn't, Mum,' she said. 'Yes, you did,' her mother replied; 'the others didn't, and they are getting a second sweet.' Jennie burst into a howl. 'But I only had one,' she cried. 'There,' said her mother, 'now you've owned it. First you steal, and then you tell a lie to cover it. Upstairs you go for the afternoon, without your doll.'

This all happened fifty years ago. 'How strict,' readers may think, 'only a little kid, and only a sweet.' Jennie, looking back, would not agree with them. She thinks that her mother by her strict ways did her children a good turn, and certainly Jennie herself could be trusted with anyone's goods.

Jennie's mother today might be labelled old-fashioned. 'Steal' is not a fashionable word. All kinds of words are used instead to describe the act of taking something which is not your own; words that make what you do appear more natural. You 'lift' something, or 'scrounge' it, or 'take it off' somebody. Readers may think of other words or phrases which are used to make stealing sound respectable. Nowadays many people resent any law which has 'you must not' in it. They mean to have their own way and appear, if possible, rather fine at the same time. Stealing, however, is stealing, by whatever name you call it.

Stealing often begins at home. Why? What reasons are there for children to feel unable to resist taking things from their parents or brothers and sisters? Why should they at times even enjoy doing it?

When Jennie stole the sweet, it was probably because she was greedy and had not learned to resist her own greed. That is a reason why many children take food and sweets from the cupboard when they think that no-one is looking. Sometimes, of course, the temptation to a little child is greater than older people know. It comes from some kind of hunger because the child is not getting the right kind of food at his meals. Readers of this book who are learning or have learned about food values should remember this when they come to have homes of their own. Children are less tempted to steal if their meals are well-balanced.

Sometimes boys and girls are tempted to steal at home —or at school—because they are trying to make up to themselves for some loss. The writer knew of a girl who was miserable after the death of her mother. She used to see things in shops which she believed would make her happy. As her pocket-money did not go far enough, she stole from her father's pockets to pay for these things.

There was a boy too (he, like the girl, was about thirteen years old) who was very lonely at home after his mother died. He saw people at school who seemed to be happy and lucky. He liked these people, but he stole from them.

Anyone who is tempted to steal because he (or she) has had a big loss should try if possible to face up to that loss. It is a real thing; you can't steal luck and happiness to make up for it. To rob other people cannot bring back a mother. Nor if she knew about the thefts would she be happy. A person who can hold on when he (or she) seems in a tunnel of unhappiness, will find, though this often seems difficult to believe, that at the end of the tunnel another kind of happiness is waiting. That is the way healthy human beings are made.

Some people today steal because they do not know the difference between right and wrong, or, if they do, do not think it matters. Two small girls (one the daughter of Jennie, now grown up) once went into a sweet shop. While Jennie's daughter was being served, she saw her companion slip a bar of chocolate-cream into her pocket. Outside, Jennie junior said, 'You took something without paying for it.' 'What of it?' said the other, 'my mother says that you must do the best you can for yourself.' Many people could give no better answer than that if they were seen stealing. How many of these people are numbered among shop-lifters?

There is a kind of stealing which really comes from jealousy. At home, a boy or girl may steal from a person in the family who seems specially favoured—father's or mother's pet. Watch the 'old' baby snatch toys from the 'new' baby, who seems to get so much attention from

Bunyan in his dream sees Christian leaving the City of Destruction for the Celestial City

mother, and you will see how it works. The 'old' baby, of course, is much too young to understand why he is behaving badly. Extra attention from older brothers or sisters is better treatment for this small thief than shaking or slaps. A distinguished general remembers how as a small boy he took sixpence deliberately from his sister's purse. She was his mother's favourite. He liked his sister, and the sixpence with him closed the account, but older boys and girls who are tempted to rob the favourite of some of his 'perks' need to think the position out for themselves, and then make their own stand against temptation.

Stealing through jealousy is easily carried outside the home. 'Why should I not take it? Look how much he (or she) has which I have not. It isn't fair!' But even if it should not be 'fair', when did two bads make a good?

Many people who are otherwise honest see no harm in robbing public bodies. They will dodge through railway barriers without a ticket, or leaving behind a ticket on which an extra sum should be paid. They will push their way off the bus as soon as the ticket-collector appears. Or they will take stationery from a Government office. Railways and the Government seem so big and wealthy; that little sum, that little amount, won't be missed. Another temptation which faces older boys and girls is to steal from their place of work. 'The firm won't miss it.' 'All the older workers do it.' Maybe that is true; but is it to the point?

One of the passages set *For study* this week is from Luke xvi. Here is a modern version of verses 10, 11.

He who is trustworthy over a little sum is trustworthy over a greater; he who plays false over a little sum, plays false over a greater; if you, then, could not be trusted to use the base riches you had, who will put the true riches into your keeping?

Those who cannot be trusted to use in an honest way money or tickets or tools, the riches of our material world, are not fit to be citizens of the Kingdom of Heaven.

Some readers may have been thinking, What about poor people? Is not poverty a reason why people steal? It is true that in past times in this country there have been people who stole for themselves or their families because they were desperate and starving, or without firing in bitter winter weather. In modern Britain people have not these frightful temptations. Of course, there are people, some old-age pensioners, for example, who have great difficulty in 'making do'; but have readers any proof that it is the poorest people who are the most grasping and dishonest? Some are among the most honest. The writer knew a pensioner, very short of money, who picked up a purse with cash in it which someone had dropped by a seat in a London park. No one saw her pick it up. She could easily have taken it home. Instead, she trudged straight to the Police Station. People far better off than she keep anything they find.

Many of us steal without meaning to do so, through the habit of borrowing. We borrow books, pencils, tools stockings. Afterwards, perhaps, we forget the book or the pencil. The tool we have borrowed seems so convenient that we hold it to use once again, and it never goes home. The stockings may be laddered and we are ashamed to return them. We don't want to have to spend money on another pair. Perhaps the owner will forget about them? Readers may suggest other 'loans' which are apt to remain with the borrowers. They may go further, and make a real effort to hand back to the owner anything borrowed by themselves—or another to replace it.

In this chapter suggestions have been made of a number of common reasons why people steal. They are not the only reasons, and readers may have suggestions of their own which they would like to add. Whatever the reason for a theft, though, a reader will find if he thinks of it that the actual theft is usually only part of the story. Do you remember Jennie? To steal that sweet she needed to be sly. To cover up the theft she lied. Stealing seldom stands alone. It is usually linked with general deceit—sly behaviour and lying. (Borrowing and not returning is more often connected with laziness.) These things may seem to pay at the time, but do they in the long run? 'Bread of deceit is sweet to a man,' says the writer of Proverbs, 'but afterwards his mouth shall be filled with gravel.'

The law of the Old Testament was, 'Thou shalt not steal'. Christ's teaching is concerned not with taking but with giving. That teaching, as found in Luke vi, may almost take our breath away, but Jesus is really saying as forcibly as possible, 'Don't haggle over possessions. Be a giver, even where it is hard to give. God does not wait for people to deserve his gifts.'

CHAPTER XIV

Before marriage

For study

The strange woman
Proverbs vii. 6-23

The marriage at Cana
John ii. 1-10

Advice from St. Paul on right living
Ephesians vi. 10-17
Philippians iv. 6, 8
Ephesians v. 1, 3-5, 8-12
1 Corinthians vi. 18-20

For extra reading

More about evil women
Proverbs vi. 20, 24-29

GOD created man in his own image, in the image of God created he him; male and female created he them. And God blessed them, and God said unto them, Be fruitful, and multiply, and replenish the earth, and subdue it. . . . And God saw everything that he had made, and behold it was very good.

These words come from the first of the two creation stories, at the opening of the book of Genesis, the book of beginnings. In the second story (chapter ii) these words occur:

Adam said [of the woman], This is now bone of my bones, and flesh of my flesh. . . . Therefore shall a man leave his father and his mother and shall cleave unto his wife; and they shall be one flesh.

There is a great deal in the Bible, in one book or another, on the proper relation between man and woman. This is bound to be so, because it is such an important matter. Of course none of the writers set out to 'explain sex'. They accepted sex differences as part of God's plan. They saw no reason to be hush-hush. Nor does a teacher of biology today, and anyone who is still in the dark on this subject should ask the teacher for a book. But the writers of the Bible were concerned with something much wider than can be found in any science text-book. They minded about men and women, how they lived, how they ought to live.

'Thou shalt not commit adultery.' Among the Commandments this is the one which deals especially with sex. Adultery is a sin of married people. To adulterate is to spoil by mixing in something else. When a married man or woman has sex relations with someone who is not his or her partner, he or she is said to commit adultery. (Someone else has mixed-up the marriage, we might say.) Jesus went further than that in his teaching, he said that if a man eyes another man's wife with desire he is committing adultery with her in his heart. He is enjoying the picture of himself doing something he ought not to do.

Readers all know something from newspapers and films about the troubles that come from broken marriages. Many know about these troubles closely, because they affect their own homes or the lives of their relations or neighbours. But how can the seventh Commandment have anything directly to do with those who are still unmarried?

The seventh Commandment can give unmarried people a warning to begin early to practise loyalty and self-control. Some boys and girls, of course, are not particularly interested in sex. They may feel superior about this, but there is no real reason to do that. Everything that we make, or do, or enjoy, uses our creative energy, that is, speaking in a general way, our sex energy. Some young people by their nature put almost every inch of their thought and strength into work, or sport, or even a favourite hobby. This gives them the advantage that they are saved, for a time at least, from having to exercise a particular kind of self-control.

Many other boys and girls are interested in those of the opposite sex, but have something in them which warns them strongly not to go too far or to cheapen themselves by 'playing at sex'. Others again find their minds easily occupied by thoughts of sex in a way that

Christian, armed to face temptation, fights a long battle against the foul fiend Apollyon

worries them. They are tempted privately by thoughts and desires which seem to them unclean, but which draw them on. Others again are quite definitely tempted to seek 'experience' with the other sex. In fact, they may think that in doing so they are showing themselves superior to their childish and strait-laced companions. The name given to sex intercourse between unmarried people is fornication.

The temptation to fornication is a very old one. It comes easily to people who have not enough to do, or who find ordinary life dull, or who have not so far found themselves particularly good at anything. It also comes easily when people are excited by dancing, some kinds of music, or even a fine night. In the passage *For study* from the book of Proverbs there is the description of a foolish youth, tempted in the evening time by a clever, experienced woman.

> At the window of my house I looked through my casement.
> And . . . I discerned among the youths, a young man void of [without] understanding.
> Passing through the street near her corner. . . .
> In the twilight, in the evening, in the black and dark night.

The woman met him and put across to him a story that 'the goodman' was away. The end?

> He goeth after her straightway, as an ox goeth to the slaughter . . . as a bird hasteth to the snare, and knoweth not that it is for his life [the deadly danger].

There is no picture in that book of a youth tempted by a young girl, perhaps in broad daylight. Nor is there one of a girl tempted by an 'experienced' older man.

Why? Girls in Eastern lands were held back from trouble—they were firmly kept at home.

The temptation to fornication was one which faced many people who joined the Christian Church in St. Paul's day. They had fallen into bad sex habits while they were still unbelievers. Afterwards, as Christians, they did not find these habits easy to give up. Here is a sentence in one of the apostle's letters (Colossians iii. 5), taken from a modern version of the Bible:

> You must deaden, then, those passions in you which belong to earth, fornication and impurity, lust and evil desire, and that love of money which is an idolatry.

Notice that St. Paul counts the temptation to fornication as one of a group of temptations towards ugly kinds of self-indulgence.

Readers may say, 'Is that fair? Sex relations between human beings are natural. You cannot compare a longing for the pleasures of sex with the greed of a miser, or love of dirty talk, or unclean habits, or cruelty, or a craving for drink.'

This may sound all right, but the object of sex relations is not just to produce a thrill. The girl who is merely out for thrills and allows herself to be used accordingly is likely to become coarse in mind and in time to look coarse. The boy who cannot resist playing at sex is liable to be labelled before long what he looks—dissipated, that is, wasted. He has wasted his manhood.

A reader may say, 'But suppose there is no question of being only out for thrills? Suppose two people are really keen on one another? Suppose that they never want to go with anyone else, enjoy the same sports, the same music, dancing together, and perhaps even mean to get married as soon as they can? Why should they not enjoy the closest sharing of all?'

Is it as simple as that? What about the deceit that may come in, the hole-in-corner ways that may be necessary? What about the plans against 'slipping-up' and bringing into the world an unwanted child? God, said the writer of the Creation story, gave the order, 'Be fruitful and multiply', and the first object of the sex act is the creation of children. But what young girl really wants a baby when she has no husband to earn for it, and perhaps no home to which she can bring it? What boy is really proud of being the father of a child when his fatherhood is marked outwardly by little more than other people's rude jokes? Besides no child really feels its parents have done the best by it if it is born out of wedlock. That brings us to the wedding.

Dearly beloved, we are gathered together here in the sight of God, and in the face of this congregation, to join together this man and this woman. . . .

That is how the marriage service of the Church of England begins. You notice, God, our families and friends, ourselves—all at our wedding. If we have 'cut our corners' before marriage, our wedding is not one at which we can happily welcome God as a guest. Yet we know that God minds about a happy wedding. As the marriage service reminds us, 'Jesus adorned and beautified' a wedding by his first miracle.

Wedding feasts in Palestine went on for several days, even till recent time. There might be a big crowd of guests, even at a village wedding. Many jars of red wine, the usual drink, had to be waiting if all were to be properly supplied. At Cana in Galilee Jesus and his disciples were guests at a wedding where wine ran short. If any of us discovered that food or drink had run short before the end of our wedding reception, we should not know where to look for shame and we should probably never forget it. To Jesus the happiness of this wedding mattered so much that, though he did not want to make himself conspicuous, he gave wine where a few moments before there had been only water.

Some people may say, 'Of course we want the best kind of wedding, but if two people are very much in love it is hard to wait'. That is true, but if two people care enough for each other, and care, too, about the children they hope to have, they will do all they can to stand up to temptation, however enticing, so that they can have the best in the end. For people who want to start off their marriage when the time comes 'on the right foot' there is a great deal of help in the Bible. Some specially useful advice is found in St. Paul's letters. He never got married himself. All his thought and energy were used in the difficult, dangerous work which he loved. But in his journeys he made friends and acquaintances of people of all sorts, both men and women. He knew how difficult it was for many of them, as it is for many people today, to keep straight. Among other things, as today, they were liable to get into trouble with their neighbours for daring to have higher standards.

Here are some pieces of advice that Paul gave at one time or another to members of the new Christian Churches. (Readers of Book Three have already studied some of the verses.)

1. Be ready at all times to make a fight for what is right. Ephesians vi. 10-17.

2. Do not worry. Take your problems and temptations to God and ask for his help (not forgetting to say 'thank you' where you ought). Philippians iv. 6.
3. Don't just decide not to think of the wrong things: think of the right ones. Philippians iv. 8.
4. Avoid bad company and sharing in any kind of unclean talk. Ephesians v. 1, 3-5, 8-12.
5. Run away from fornication. Paul explains in 1 Corinthians vi. 18, 19, why this must be so. If we commit fornication we are offending against our own bodies. They are not just bodies, but the homes of our spirits, which belong to God through the power of the Holy Spirit. They are, in Paul's words, 'temples of the Holy Ghost', and so must be kept clean.

People who can get into the way of right thinking and put up a good fight for self-control are not only likely to reach the best kind of wedding day: they are likely to be able to build a married life which is not easily broken.

CHAPTER XV

Thou shalt not kill

For study

Cain and Abel

Genesis iv. 3-11
1 John iii. 11, 12, 15

Joseph and his brothers

Genesis xxxvii. 3, 4, 12-14, 18-27

Moses' vengeance

Exodus ii. 11-12

Love your brother, neighbour, and enemy

Leviticus xix. 17, 18
Matthew v. 43-45

A picture of love

1 Corinthians xiii. 4-7
('charity' = 'love')

For extra reading

Judgement of David

2 Samuel xii. 1-10

God's love and ours

1 John iv. 10-12, 18-21

Help the ass of friend or foe

Deuteronomy xxii. 4
Exodus xxiii. 4, 5

THE first murder story in the Bible is the story of two brothers, Cain and Abel. The reason for the murder was jealousy. God, the writer says (though why we cannot be certain), valued Abel's offering more than Cain's. The elder brother hated the younger one because he had the better standing with God, so he killed him.

In the well-known story of Joseph and his brethren, jealousy shows up too. The older brothers were jealous of their young brother because their father Jacob loved him better than any of them. They envied Joseph too, for his father gave him the long-sleeved robe ('coat of many colours') which showed that he wished him to be his heir. Envy of Joseph's position and prospects, jealousy of his father's regard for him: these joined to make some of the brothers ready to kill him out of hand, others at least eager never to see him again.

A person can be guilty of murder as a result of covetousness. This is, perhaps, specially the case where sex comes in. King David coveted Bathsheba the wife of Uriah. Her husband, readers may remember, was away from home, serving in the king's army. The king took her, and when her husband was recalled on leave, and it looked as if the king's behaviour would appear in a bad light, David got rid of him by a trick. For all this, the prophet Nathan told David, God would punish him.

Jealousy, envy, covetousness: these can lead to murder. Then there is the kind of hate that we connect with nationalism, the hate known by people who feel themselves held in, or trodden down, by another power. There is a story in the book of Exodus about Moses when he was a young man. Moses had for himself nothing to complain of. He had been adopted by an Egyptian princess and had received the best of everything, clothes, food, education. But his sympathy was with his own Hebrew people, oppressed by the Egyptians. One day when he saw an Egyptian beating a Hebrew he gave vent to his bottled-up hatred. He murdered the Egyptian and hid his body in the sand.

All these stories from the Old Testament which tell of hatred are easily understood by people of today. Some of us know what it is to be jealous of the brother or sister who seems to get more than a fair share of our father or mother's attention. ('Sometimes I could kill the little brute.') Some of us know that murderous feeling when a boy or girl friend, whom we had thought was specially ours, prefers another person to ourselves. Some of us feel envy for the person who seems to be able to do easily things in work or sports which to ourselves seem almost impossibly difficult. We find ourselves describing these people by such words as 'smug' or 'slick' or 'teacher's pet'. Again, from newspapers we know of the hatreds which are aroused by nationalism, or the colour bar. We read too of group hatreds, workers for employers, or strikers for 'black-legs'.

Sometimes we read of a murder such as this: a man enters a house or shop at night, intending to rob. He is surprised by the owner, gets into a panic, strikes out crazily, and kills the person who has found him. Fear is at the back of that murder, the fear of the thief for his own skin. (A great many soldiers who are trigger-happy are not so because they are bold fighters, but because they are 'jumpy'. It is the frightened man who in jungle fighting endangers his comrades by 'letting-off' where he should be still and watchful.)

Sometimes, of course, thieves will carry out a cold-blooded murder of a person who stands in their way. These people may be more heartless than afraid.

Murder, then, may come about as the consequence of ugly feelings such as jealousy, envy, hatred, or fear. Or it may come because the murderer sees a person only as a thing to be got out of his way.

The Old Testament teaches that murder, the taking of another person's life, is against the law of God. What is Christ's teaching? He says:

> You have heard how the men of old were told, '*Murder not*:
> whoever murders must come up for sentence,
> whoever maligns [speaks evil of] his brother must come before the Sanhedrin,
> whoever curses his brother must go to the fire of Gehenna [hell].'
> But I tell you, whoever is angry with his brother [without cause] will be sentenced by God.

This quotation is from a modern version of Matthew v. 21, 22. In our Authorized Version the arrangement does not make Christ's meaning really clear. 'Without cause' was probably not in the original. Christ is saying, 'Don't be angry. Don't have murderous thoughts, God knows what is in your heart and judges you accordingly.'

This teaching is, clearly, very difficult to follow, even if by 'brother' is meant only one's brother by blood. We can easily be filled with jealousy, envy, or rage against members of our own family. We can even hate them through fear. But 'brother' in the Bible means more than that. It may include relations and neighbours and other people of your own race.

Here are lines from the book of Leviticus:

> Thou shalt not hate thy brother in thine heart. . . .
> Thou shall not avenge, nor bear any grudge against the children of thy people, but thou shalt love thy neighbour as thyself: I am the Lord.

In parts of the Old Testament room is left for hatred of people of other races, but when we come to the New Testament, Christ's teaching does not allow hatred of anyone at all:

> You have heard the saying: '*You must love your neighbour* and hate your enemy'. But I tell you, love your enemies and pray for those who persecute you, that you may be sons of your Father in heaven.

Is Christ expecting impossibilities? Can people really love their enemies? It is certainly very, very difficult. Most of us find it hard enough to be glad if we hear anything good about them. Yet to go further than that has not proved impossible. Here, for example, is the story of a young seaman.

On Sunday, April 8th, 1945, during the Second World War, the press bureau of the Chief of the S.S. (Hitler's Guard) and the police force in Denmark issued this announcement:

> Condemned to death: Seaman Kim Malthe-Bruun, born on July 8th, 1923, in Saskatchewan, Canada, resident in Copenhagen, because as a member of an illegal organization he annexed a revenue service boat and took it to Sweden. In addition he procured arms for his organization and took part in transporting arms. The death sentence was carried out by a firing squad.

Lions in the way on the hill Difficulty. The porter cries out that they are chained

Though Kim had been born in Canada, he was a German citizen. He hated Hitler's brutal government, and had managed from a base in Sweden to help to bring arms to people who were ready to fight to overthrow it. Then just before Christmas 1944, he found himself in the hands of the Gestapo, Hitler's police. His courage did not fail—nor did his pride. He felt scorn for his captors. In a letter which was smuggled out of the prison he called those who questioned and abused him 'dregs of humanity'. Then, as he sat locked within four walls, he gave his mind to the New Testament. He saw that proud people today are like the Pharisees. They know the teaching of the Scriptures only from outside, as words, not as something to be lived. As Kim studied, suddenly, time and again, behind the teaching he saw Jesus himself. It was not what we call a vision, more an understanding, as we understand our friends. He realized that it is no use to try to follow Jesus' teaching as if it were a set of rules. We must, as it were, join up with him, support him from the bottom of our heart.

Some days later Kim was tortured and brought back unconscious to his cell. Afterwards he was surprised to find that though his body was still afraid—his heart beat faster every time someone stopped at his door—his soul was not afraid. He felt no hatred of the people who tortured him. Even more than that he understood Jesus' love for everyone, including quite specially those who crucified him.

A reader may ask, 'As Kim began to understand "loving your enemies", did he become ashamed of the days when he had joined in gun-running?' The answer is, 'No, apparently not'. When he joined the 'Underground' he did what he believed to be right. He risked his life to help people who were fighting for freedom against a cruel and wicked government. Like many keen young people, Kim acted as seemed right at the moment, and did not go back on it. He had to follow his own road to Christian faith. In prison, perhaps we might say, he climbed quickly and steeply to a higher point on his road, nearer to the Celestial City. But looking back, he wrote in his last letter to his mother, 'I travelled a road that I have never regretted'.

Suppose Kim had lived on? Suppose he had had to try to carry out the teaching of Jesus in the ordinary workaday world? He might, like the rest of us, have found it very difficult. As it was, a month after he was tortured he was condemned to death. He thought of his girl-friend, of the times they had together, and the years which lay ahead of her when he would not be there. Then he wrote to her. He did not beseech her after the fashion of the dying soldier-lover in the old German song:

> O, love, dear love, be true.
> Be only, only mine.

Instead, he urged his girl not to remain sorrowful. She must remember their love for each other as something golden; but she must go forward to new things. One day he hoped she would meet the man who was to be her husband and be 'very, very happy'. He signed his letter, 'Yours, but not forever, Kim'.

This young man, we might say, had been given a short course in love as Jesus understands it. It allows no room for grasping at things for yourself, for hate or envy or jealousy. Maybe Kim before he died understood 1 Corinthians xiii. 4, 5 better than most of us.

CHAPTER XVI

Thou shalt not bear false witness

For study

A faked trial
1 Kings xxi. 9-13

The law of witness and false witness
Deuteronomy xix. 15-21

Witnesses at Christ's trial
Matthew xxvi. 57-62

'Destroy this temple'
John ii. 13-21

A man of God
Psalm xv

For extra reading

Witnesses at Stephen's trial
Acts vi. 8-14

Christian behaviour
Colossians iii. 1, 2, 9, 13, 14

'DON'T tell lies about other people.' Why should anyone want to do so? Before going further, suppose the reader pauses to write down, say, four reasons which he or she might give. Perhaps some of these reasons may be the same as those suggested later in this chapter.

The words of the Commandment which form the heading of this chapter may lead at once to questions. A false witness: is that anyone who tells lies about others? Surely, witnesses are people who give evidence at trials? Of course, the witness at the trial is a person who can most obviously do harm to another by telling lies or half-lies. That shows in the most famous trial stories in the Bible.

One well-known Old Testament trial story is that of Naboth. Readers may remember that Naboth was given a faked trial. He had no chance from the beginning. The queen, Jezebel, wanted to get rid of him in such a fashion that his property would be handed over to the king, her husband. So she ordered the elders of the city to accuse Naboth of treason. Two men, 'Sons of Belial' (which means 'sons of worthlessness' or 'worthless fellows'), were employed as witnesses to say that Naboth had blasphemed God and the king. According to Jewish law, the evidence of two witnesses who exactly agreed was enough on which to convict a man. Naboth was found guilty and put to death.

These 'sons of worthlessness' probably gave false witness simply for money. The bribing of witnesses in Eastern lands is not unusual to this very day.

But what of the elders, supposed to be so respectable? Technically speaking, of course, they were not witnesses, but they put the lies into the men's mouths. Why did they do it? Clearly they were frightened of the queen. They sacrificed Naboth to save themselves.

The most famous trial story of all is told in each of the Gospels, the trial of Jesus Christ before the Jewish Council. In the account given in Matthew xxvi. 57-62, we read of 'many false witnesses' who disagree with each other and two who agree on one story. Readers should note what they say, in verses 60 and 61, and then turn to John ii. 13-21. Here the occasion of which they are speaking is explained and the real words of Jesus are given. The two witnesses agreed on a half-truth, just as damaging as a straight lie.

At the trial of Jesus why should all these people come forward with false witness? In general, of course, they knew that their national leaders, the chief priests and the Jewish Council, hated Jesus. Even if they meant to stick to the letter of the law in judging him, they would be delighted to hear all the bad things. Some of the witnesses, no doubt, themselves hated Jesus, as a revolutionary, a dangerous fellow. Given a chance, they believed, he would change things, do away with old customs. Then there were the people who had been making money by trade in the Temple. Jesus had attacked them and their dishonest trade. They must have been terrified that he would upset their business, and they would lose their profits. Both these groups of people had what is called today 'a vested interest' in getting rid of Jesus. Other false witnesses may have been people who wanted to be popular with the Jewish leaders and thought that by speaking evil of Jesus they would be so. Others again may have been the kind who are prepared to say anything if only it will get them into the public eye. The police today have to cope with many people who after an accident long to come forward as a witness. Sometimes these people have never seen the accident at all. They were at the other end of the street, or the other side of the house. But they persuade themselves, and try to persuade others, that they must have been there.

Those who study the trial of Stephen, described in Acts vi. 9-14, will find again the 'many false witnesses'. They will find too the garbled tale about Jesus and the destruction of the Temple. The atmosphere at this trial seems rather the same as at the trial of Stephen's Master.

In connection with the three trials studied, six reasons for false witness have been suggested. Here they are summarized:

(*a*) To get money.
(*b*) To save yourself at someone else's expense.
(*c*) Dislike of the other person's ideas (not only in religion but in such things as politics).
(*d*) Fear of the other person's power to spoil your business.
(*e*) To make yourself popular with people you admire (or fear) by running down the other person to them.
(*f*) To get notice for yourself by speaking at the trial.

If readers look at them carefully, they will see that all might also be reasons for telling lies about people in ordinary life. Here is one example for each:

(*a*) A man runs down another man's firm or his work to get the contract or the 'fat' job for himself.

(*b*) A child says, untruly, 'He did it. I never!'

(*c*) Someone says, 'Yes, the fellow teaches a lot of dangerous stuff. Why, at the meeting (or the service) last week they say that he said . . .' Here follows something heard at third hand, through people who dislike the speaker or preacher.

(*d*) A shopkeeper says, 'Yes, of course Jones has a wonderful window, much more attractive than ours, but . . .' Here follows a suggestion that you haven't seen the state of the place at the back, or that, of course, people can do these things if they don't mind about paying the bills—something that will 'smear' the rival whom the shopkeeper fears.

(*e*) A boy or girl tells lies to a bully about another boy or girl who has had the courage to stand up to the bully.

(*f*) A small boy finds his parents occupied with their own business and not attending to him, so he invents a yarn about an accident he saw at the corner of the road. A girl (or boy) invents a story about herself (himself) and her (his) conquests, which will draw the attention from other girls (or boys) to herself (or himself).

Readers may have other examples in mind under any of the six headings. Or they may have listed further reasons why people are tempted to tell lies about others. Jealousy is a likely one. Then there is the dislike that you simply cannot explain, the dislike shown in the old rhyme:

I do not love thee, Dr. Fell—
The reason why I cannot tell;
But this alone I know full well,
I do not love thee, Dr. Fell.

Perhaps the reason most likely to be suggested for telling lies is the love of gossip. Gossip, of course, can be pleasant and harmless, but easily turns into the kind of talebearing that means lies or half-lies.

'Thou shalt not go up and down as a talebearer among thy people.' These words from the Book of Leviticus (chapter xix) are part of the Jewish Law. We can all understand why such a law should be necessary, even though we have seen nothing worse than the kind of talebearing that goes on among children in the Primary School. Like a good deal of grown-up gossip, it is often spiced with the wish to get someone else into trouble.

He fosters good feeling who keeps quiet about some wrong:
the man who gossips about it divides friend from friend—

these words are from a modern version of Proverbs xvii. 9. Even if there is something wrong, the writer believes, talk about it is likely to do more harm than good. His words can usefully be remembered by the person who is tempted to tell one of those pieces of gossip which begin, 'I think you ought to know'.

During the Second World War a woman was left by her soldier husband at home with her four children. She was still young and pretty; she had married when she was scarcely sixteen. Life was dull. Food was rationed; clothes were rationed. It was difficult to make ends meet. At one time the children got measles. She toiled up regularly to the hospital with any fruit and sweets she could get, and smiled and waved at them through the glass partition as they lay in bed; but she longed for a good time.

After her husband had been away for more than two years, the wife was tempted to get some fun by going to dances. A man with whom she danced paid her attention. Neighbours began to talk. Suddenly she heard that her husband was demobilized; he was coming home. She also learned that someone had written him one of those letters which begin, 'I think you ought to know'. She knew that her husband was hard and very jealous. What would he think and do? She was so terrified that she persuaded the man with whom she had been dancing to run away with her. Without warning, she left her home and her children for ever. When the children woke up one morning she simply was not there.

What was the person who wrote the letter beginning 'I think you ought to know' really trying to do? Readers might think that out. What he or she did was, first, to scare a foolish little woman into going away with a man who would never respect her, and, secondly, to leave two girls and two boys without a mother. The eldest, a girl, was just fifteen and small like her mother. She remembers how, in the days that followed, her own tears would add to the dampness of things as she struggled with soaking sheets, trying to do the week's wash in the way that her mother would have done.

There is a proverb which says:

> Only a base man listens to malicious words;
> only the false attend to mischievous talk.

The father of that family would have been very angry if anyone had called him base or false; but his wife knew that he was one of those people who would listen, would attend. He was not, though he was thought respectable, really the sort of man for whom God is looking.

Lord, who shall abide in thy tabernacle? who shall dwell in thy holy hill?

A psalmist asks that question and gives his own answer. Here is the first part of it:

He that walketh uprightly, and worketh righteousness, and speaketh the truth in his heart.

He that backbiteth not with his tongue, nor doeth evil to his neighbour, nor taketh up a reproach against [believes ill of] his neighbour.

Notice the psalmist's points. The man who comes closest to God is honest in thought and deed. To his neighbour he does nothing hurtful in word, deed, or thought. For him false witness of any kind is out of the question.

CHAPTER XVII

'If only I had . . .'

For study

Nothing goes with you

Job i. 20, 21
Psalm xlix. 16-20
Luke xii. 15-20

Content or covetous?

1 Timothy vi. 6-12

Things which are worth while

Luke xii. 22, 23, 29-31
1 Corinthians xii. 31 and xiii. 13
('charity' = 'love')
Mark viii. 34-37

For extra reading

God and our lives

Psalm xc. 1-4, 10-12, 16-17

'IF only I had . . .' We all say this at times. Some people say it often. If only I had A's money, or B's car, or C's 'telly'. If only I had X's good looks, or Y's brains, or Z's power of getting away with it. If only I had this or that, I should be perfectly happy.

Of course this is not true. A famous doctor who was working in Switzerland once wrote about the wealthy people who came to him for advice. They came from all over Europe and from America too. They came because he was a specially skilled 'nerve' doctor and they were miserable and depressed. They told him their troubles. One trouble was this, the patient was so bored with life. Some of the men had enjoyed themselves making big money. Some of the women had enjoyed spending it. These people had been able to buy the best of everything, clothes, houses, cars, and yachts. They could afford the most expensive tickets for the best shows and the most expensive kind of holiday. Now they were suffering from a feeling that there was nothing that money could buy that was really worth while. Some felt this extra deeply because their personal life seemed to have gone to pieces. Their marriage had broken up, or they had lost someone they loved, a son or a daughter, a husband or a wife. Life without the lost person did not make sense. Others knew that someone for whom they cared was ill with a fatal disease, and that the day was creeping near when they would be left alone. Some were beginning to feel old. What was left to look forward to, they wanted to know.

These people had everything that money could buy. Many of them were good-looking and clever too, yet they were completely miserable. What, after all, had they to look forward to? There is one straight, hard answer which you can find in both the Old and New Testaments. Look first for it in Job's words when he was told that all his property, all his family, had been carried off or destroyed (Job i. 21). Here is the same idea expressed in a modern version of part of Psalm xlix:

> So fear not when a man grows rich,
> and when the splendour of his house increases;
> he can take nothing with him when he dies,
> his splendour will not follow him below. . . .
> For all the splendour that they cherish,
> men pass, even as the beasts that perish.

Both Job and the psalmist realized that our bodies belong, like our goods, to the earth. Both pass.

Now turn to the New Testament, Luke xii. 16-21, and read what Jesus had to say in his story of the prosperous farmer, about people who stake their happiness on the things which they possess. He makes the same point: it is no good to pin our happiness to our possessions, or the enjoyment of possessions. We cannot take them to the grave. Our soul goes forth alone.

A reader may say, 'That is true; but is it necessary to be so gloomy? Our position is different. We are still young. Most of us are unlikely ever to be rich enough to have everything that we want. But after all, we have only one life. Why should we not try to get everything that we can that will make it enjoyable?'

Jesus gives a direct answer to this, which you can find in Luke xii. 15. Here are the words in a modern version:

> He said to them, look well and keep yourselves clear of all covetousness. A man's life does not consist in having more possessions than he needs.

Mr. Worldly Wiseman suggests a different goal, a comfortable and respectable village

Life, in fact, is not just a matter of having things, of doing as well or better than the Jones', as we say today.

Later Jesus explains that God knows the things that we need, such as clothes, food, and drink. These things for us should have second place while we seek God's Kingdom.

Now this is where things often, especially to young people, begin to seem unreal. Valuing God's Kingdom above all earthly things, what does that in practice mean? Perhaps those rich people who had lost someone they loved had an inkling. Perhaps some of them felt, 'I would give up all that I possess to have that person back again'. They had found that people matter more than things, that caring and being cared for by someone was more important to them than anything else. If any of them had studied the Bible, they might remember that St. Paul advised Christians to 'covet earnestly the best gifts' and that he showed that the best gift of all is love. People who have grasped that love matters more than anything else in the world have made a good beginning towards putting God's Kingdom first. Of course, as long as they think that this is just a matter of having the one person that you want, they have not got far. Love between two people can work out as a form of selfishness-between-two.

The writer remembers hearing of a house where visitors at meal-times did not enjoy themselves. The husband and wife (they had no children) were always so busy seeing that the other one had whatever he or she wanted. The guest had to sit there, longing for the marmalade, perhaps, or the mustard, or another slice of bread, and watch the couple looking after each other.

The love of which St. Paul spoke was a much wider affair than this. It was the kind of love that Jesus showed in his life on earth. He gave up the comforts of a settled village home and a skilled trade, to take what came along while he gave his attention to other people, teaching, healing, comforting. That meant days surrounded by crowds who might be out for what they could get, dirty and diseased. It might mean chilly nights in the open with wild animals around. To make clear to us what God's love means, Jesus risked his life among men who hated him. Finally he gave up his life in the service of God's Kingdom.

Jesus put God first all the way. Many of the unhappy people who visited the famous doctor had been like the prosperous farmer of the story. That had put wealth first and things which wealth brings, comfort and pleasure. They had given, St. Paul might have said, first place to an idol. Do you remember that covetousness, or the love of money, he called idolatry? (See page 122.) The writer of the first Epistle to Timothy calls it 'the root of all evil' or 'a root from which every kind of evil springs'. Here is his comment in a modern version:

> Those who would be rich fall into temptation, the devil's trap for them; all those useless and dangerous appetites [desires] which sink men into ruin here and perdition [destruction] hereafter. The love of money is a root from which every kind of evil springs, and there are those who have wandered away from the faith by making it their ambition, involving themselves in a world of sorrows.

'A world of sorrows?' In such sadness some of the doctor's wealthy patients in the end found themselves. They went, late on, to see what a doctor could do to help them to mend their lives. Servants of God, as the writer of the Epistle goes on to show, need to take a different road from the beginning:

> It is for thee, servant of God, to shun all this; to aim at right living, holiness and faith and love and endurance and kind forbearance. Fight the good fight of faith, lay thy grasp on eternal life.

Eternal life is the life where doing right matters more than getting rich, where people matter more than things, where other people matter more than yourself. The citizen of God's Kingdom desires to be a good citizen of earth, of course, but that does not necessarily mean a wealthy one. He is one who is strictly honest in business, able to be trusted with the club accounts or the employer's goods. He is the kind of person who is welcome at home too, known to make the best of things and people. The covetous person can be a disturbing member of a business: 'How can I wangle to do best for myself?' He can be a disturbing member of a family: 'Why not more pocket-money?' Why (later on) should he hand over so much of his pay-packet for his keep? All these things apply also to many a 'she'.

Compare the covetous person with the old doctor, of whom a mother said that in bad times he seemed 'like hope coming into the house'. Compare him with the district nurse who is never out of patience; or the boy who never fails to see the funny side as long as there is one; or the gardener who has never been beaten by a job yet; or the man who is such a good neighbour, and, better still, never talks of it. It is these people, not the person who believes he would be happy if he only had X, who know something of eternal life.

CHAPTER XVIII

God above all

For study

God first

Matthew xxii. 35-40

Praise to God the Creator

Psalm cxxxvi. 1-9, 25, 26

Wild scarlet anemones (not our lilies)

Matthew vi. 28, 29

The righteous God

Deuteronomy x. 12, 13, 17, 18
James i. 16, 17, 19, 20, 26, 27

For extra reading

Service of God

Psalm xxxiv. 11-22

WHAT do we do to enter into life? Keep the Comments, Jesus taught, those which come in under the great law, 'Thou shalt love thy neighbour as thyself'. He did not speak of those Commandments which are concerned with behaviour towards God. He knew, no one better, that of course God comes first, but that most of us learn the meaning of love in ordinary, human ways. He understood that it is easier to love, say, one of our family than anyone so remote as God seems to be. He understood, too, that the selfish, self-satisfied young man who has not even learned to love his brother is talking nonsense when he says he loves God. When, however, one of the scribes asked Jesus the question, 'Which is the great commandment in the Law?' he answered at once in the words which he had known since he was a little boy:

> Thou shalt love the Lord thy God with all thy heart, and with all thy soul, and with all thy mind.
> This is the first and great commandment.

This 'great commandment' covers all those Commandments among the Ten which deal with our behaviour to God. Which are they, and what are we asked to do?

Look at the first Commandment (see page 103). It tells us that we must give honour to God alone. What does that mean in practice?

To the people who earliest knew the Ten Commandments, it meant that they must give honour to a God who belonged specially to them and had helped them, not to the gods of other tribes. But, as Part One has shown, by the time that the book of Job was written the Jews knew better than that. To Job, God is the ruler of the mysterious and at times terrifying world in which men live, and of the stars in the high heaven beyond. He is righteous and just too, though his ways are far beyond man's understanding.

To the Christian, God is even more: he is our Father, the Father of our Lord Jesus Christ, and one of his names is love.

What can we do to show that this God is our God, if we are Christians? All kinds of things, as earlier study has shown. Before going further, readers might try to decide their own answers. Perhaps their answers will agree with some of the suggestions made below.

One way in which we can show that God is our God is to give him honour in words; by hymns, or psalms of praise in church or chapel or school.

> Praise my soul, the King of heaven;
> To his feet thy tribute bring.
> Ransomed, healed, restored, forgiven,
> Who like me his praise should sing?
> Praise him! Praise him!
> Praise the everlasting King.

There you have a straightforward hymn of praise.

We can show honour to God the Creator by having respect for the things in nature which he has made. Take this example. Many people who enter a bluebell wood in spring are amazed by its loveliness, but they do not see the loveliness as part of the miracle of God's creation and treat it gently. Instead, they try to snatch the loveliness for themselves. They trample into the wood and pull up bluebells by hundreds. They leave behind them broken stems and crushed flowers, even if they do not also leave ragged boughs where they have wrenched off young branches. Home they go with great bundles of flagging flowers. Of course, to take a few flowers and leaves skilfully does not spoil a wood, and they may help to make home or the office or school look pleasant. They are a reminder of the holiday too. But to snatch at and destroy beautiful things is no service to God the Creator. Readers may be able to suggest other examples of ways in which people carelessly destroy things more beautiful than man could ever make.

Another way of keeping the first Commandment, the command to worship a God who is righteous, must surely be to try and act rightly, to bring to God as far as we can the offering of right living. This, readers may remember, Job tried to do. One of his troubles was, though, that he brought himself too much into the picture and thought that God ought to recognize his goodness and not reward him with so much suffering.

God our Father; perhaps the most obvious way in which we can show that we worship him is that we pay attention to him. We can listen to his voice when it speaks to us in our conscience, or perhaps in other ways, sometimes in the things we hear in church or school, that stick in our minds. We can speak to him in our prayers. We have the Lord's Prayer as a pattern. Very few of us give God our Father the attention that we should. We are inclined to use him as selfish children use their parents, as someone to whom they can run when things go wrong. There are people who have none of our helps who worship him better than we do.

Amy Carmichael, of whom readers of *Servants of God at Work* already know, tells in one of her books of an

Indian girl called Mimosa. Her father was a Hindu. Members of his caste count themselves as belonging to the god Siva, one of the best-known Indian nature gods. Mimosa's father worked hard to fulfil the rules of his religion, but he was one of those thoughtful Hindus who are really searching for the God beyond all gods, 'the Supreme'. Who was this Supreme? Mimosa's sister Star had believed that he was worshipped by the Christians. She had run away to join Miss Carmichael, and her father had never felt able to remove her, though several times he had gone meaning to fetch her away. So Star had stayed and learned the whole Christian faith. But Mimosa only once, one afternoon, heard about 'a living, loving God, whom we call Father, who made everything in the world, and the sun, moon and stars'. She wanted to know more, to stay with Miss Carmichael, but her father would not hear of it, and home she went with him.

Something had happened to Mimosa, though. She was quite sure that what she had heard was true. God was there, everywhere, and he loved her. The results were disturbing to her family. She would no longer mark her forehead each morning with the sacred ashes of Siva. When her angry mother punished her, Mimosa still refused. She was puzzled that her loving God allowed her to suffer because she served him, but she still hung on to her faith in him.

Her father died; and Mimosa's life was harder still. Her mother married her to a man who proved to be up to the neck in debt, lazy and foolish. In time all her dowry was gone, the land, the jewels, even her brass cooking-pots. Sometimes her husband worked, more often she had herself to work in the fields to keep him and their little boys. Her neighbours scorned her: they thought her foolish to worry about the debts; they said that her troubles came because she broke the customs of her caste.

Whatever happened, though, Mimosa was sure that God her Father knew of her troubles and would never really forsake her. One night there was no food in the house, but her hungry boys knelt with her to worship God before they fell asleep. Then she knelt before her Father, holding out one of the folds of her sari (draped dress) as if she was waiting for a gift from him. 'If the gardener has to water a great many little plants', she said, 'will he not sometimes forget one little plant? My children and I are your plants. I think, perhaps, you have forgotten us tonight. But never mind. Shall I be offended with you? Only I ask you to be as the hen with her little chickens. Gather us under your wings.'

It was nearly midnight when Mimosa finished her prayer. The village lay dark and sleeping. Then she heard footsteps which stopped at her door. A voice said, 'Sister'. She opened the door and saw outside the figure of a middle-aged man, her cousin. 'Hast thou any food? Have the children any food?' he asked. He was carrying a brass vessel heaped with rice and vegetable curry, the Hindu's chief food. Something, he could not say what, had prevented him from going to sleep until he had carried out this errand.

In time Mimosa was able to stay with Amy Carmichael and hear in words things which she had been discovering for herself. Quite soon she was counted ready for baptism. Is that surprising? Only one afternoon's lesson had been needed to set her feet firmly on a road to Christian faith through the worship of God her Father.

One thing that this Indian girl grasped from the beginning was that God should be honoured by faithful work. It was the way she worked in his own fields that first brought her to the notice of the cousin who helped her by night. To serve God by faithful work is open to all of us.

'Thou shalt have no other gods before me.' Suppose we do all the things mentioned in this chapter: sing God's praise, have respect for his creation, pray to him trustfully, try to live rightly and work faithfully, as in his sight. Is it possible for us still to put another 'god' in a higher place? Read Chapter XIX before you decide the answer.

CHAPTER XIX

Idols and oaths

For study

The image

Isaiah xliv. 14-17, 19

God and idols

Psalm cxv. 1-8

Worship of God alone

Deuteronomy vi. 13, 14
Luke iv. 1-8

The false oath

Leviticus xix. 12

For extra reading

God and the image makers

Isaiah xliv. 6, 8, 9

Avoiding oaths

Matthew v. 33-37

THE second Commandment, 'Thou shalt not make unto thee any graven image'. How can that apply to us? We are not tempted to worship nature gods as the Israelites were. Of course there are mascots and gremlins. How many of us seriously believe that they are any use? Still, what about having one on the desk or in the cockpit of the plane, 'just in case'?

To rely on mascots and gremlins might be called a feeble kind of worshipping graven images. A woollen doll, a black cat, a sketched-out face and hands, what can they do? To some people to have them there seems to satisfy a superstitious part of their nature. These things are like the fetishes that primitive people carry, tied round their necks, to preserve them, as they think, from evil spirits. The mascots are supposed to be symbols of some power that will protect the wearer. But what power? When we attach importance to things made of wool and wire and paper we are behaving rather like the man of whom Isaiah of Babylon wrote. He cuts down a tree and uses part of the wood for a fire to warm himself. He roasts his meat before it, and on the hot ashes he bakes his bread. The rest of the tree he makes into a god, falls down before it and asks it to save him.

People take to mascots when they are afraid—afraid of failing in an examination, afraid that their plane may crash. A person who believes in God's protecting care has no reason for fear. Look at Matthew x. 28-31.

Another way in which we can break the second Commandment is by making a god of some person or thing.

A girl known to the writer of this book almost made a god of hockey (she played very well). During school classes she often managed to get away with half-attention while she watched the window. What hope of the weather holding out for the afternoon's game or match? (Plenty of us may have done this!) On Saturdays she was ready to cut home duties to get off early to hockey. She even said that if she died she would not be happy in heaven if there were no hockey there. Perhaps she was unusual. More often girls are content to dream away their working-time thinking of their favourite film or TV star. Others make themselves, their clothes and make-up, the centre of the picture. This applies to some boys, bar, of course, the make-up. Then there are boys who are such football fans that they almost seem to make gods of their chosen team. They will let anybody and anything suffer rather than miss a match or the sports news. Other boys might be said to make a graven image of a motor-bicycle. They think of nothing else.

Stars and clothes, sport and possessions. These are some of the things that should be enjoyed but not made into gods.

When people are older, they may make other false gods. Some women make gods of their houses. The writer remembers one house which was spotless, even to the floors; but only because no member of the family, however late or tired, was allowed across the threshold till outdoor shoes were changed for clean slippers.

Men more often make a god of money. A certain man once told the writer, 'I believe in big money'. For a time this man seemed to have chosen his god wisely. He became very wealthy. He could afford rooms for himself and his wife in the most comfortable hotels. They had

Hopeful encourages Christian in the river of death. Shining figures from the Celestial City await them

first-class cabins on transatlantic liners. They were able to visit the loveliest places in Europe and America. Then this man had symptoms of a terrible disease. He knew about it; he had seen someone he cared for die of it many years before. He could afford the best treatment, but he knew that it was unlikely that any known treatment could in the end save his life. He had no longer any interest in making money. The pleasure had gone from spending it. Money had let him down.

What does the reader think that he (or she) would have done at this point? The sick man did this; he said that he was not going to believe that he had the disease. If he refused to believe it was there, he said, it would not be there.

The man's wife urged him to have an operation. She was very fond of him, and she hoped that the operation might give him, anyhow, a longer lease of life. He would not listen to her, and she sat beside him day by day during the months in which he lay dying.

This man did not mean to dishonour God, but on his road through life he had, without realizing it, turned aside to worship a graven image. (Readers who have forgotten the warning given in 1 Timothy vi, about the dangers which come from the love of money, should look back to page 147.) If, like Christian in *Pilgrim's Progress*, he had kept his face turned towards the place where his king dwelt, the Celestial City, in what ways might his story have been different? Look back and see if you can decide on at least three differences.

There are other ways of worshipping a 'god of this world'. One of the passages set *For study* is taken from the mysterious story of Christ's temptations. He was offered by Satan all that the world could give—at a price. His refusals came at once, from the Bible (in verses *For study*, from Psalm xci and Deuteronomy vi).

The third Commandment is one that older people often break through what might be called a bad habit. They may be good-living people, who believe that they have a respect for their Maker, but if they live or work among people who use the name of God or of Christ in bad language, they get accustomed to hearing it. Next, they use the language themselves without thinking what it means. Boys and girls can, if they want to, check themselves at the beginning from taking God's name in vain, or joining in silly or ugly language about serious things. Some readers may have noticed already how difficult it is, though, to avoid being cowardly on this subject. Many people will not allow their friends to speak rudely about members of their family, even though, privately, they may think that there are a number of things wrong at home. Yet those same people will not stand up for the honour of God, though they believe he is good and they count him their helper. Readers of *Servants of God at Work* may remember how Dr. Grenfell called those who really believed in God and Christ, and let other people make fun of their religion, 'weak-kneed Christians'.

There is a specially deliberate form of taking God's name in vain which is connected with law courts. It is called perjury, or a false oath. The person swears before Almighty God that he will speak the truth, when he is prepared to tell any lie that suits his purpose. This is rightly counted in law a punishable offence. Jesus taught that we should not need to promise anything on oath. Our word, the word of an honest person, should be enough.

CHAPTER XX

The rest day

For study

The Sabbath

Exodus xx. 8-11

A Sabbath at Capernaum

Mark i. 21-31

Another Sabbath

Mark ii. 23-28
Mark iii. 1-5

The praise of God in his house

Psalm c. 1-5

For extra reading

Friday; the Sabbath; Sunday

Luke xxiii. 50-56
Luke xxiv. 1-6

Another psalm of praise

Psalm cxxxviii. 1-8

THE fourth Commandment. Read it straight through in Exodus xx. 8-11. 'Remember', it says, 'to keep holy the Sabbath day.' So it begins with a reminder, not of something we must not do but of something we must do. It goes on to say that every seventh day is to be for man and beast a Sabbath, a day of rest from work. God, so tells the ancient poem at the opening of Genesis, after the six days of his work of creation rested the seventh day. He blessed that day of rest and set it apart as holy, as his special day.

The people of Israel, to whom the Commandment was given, prized their Sabbath. Many Jews still prize it to-day. It is called 'the beloved', the best day of the week. Jewish families all over the world welcome its coming each Friday at sundown with a special meal. The house is in order, all cooking has been done. The family are wearing their best clothes, and the mother has lighted the Sabbath lamp.

Since the resurrection of Jesus Christ on the first day of the week, Sunday has become to Christians the week's holy day. How should it be used? Should we spend it as the Jews spend their Sabbath? If so, what would that mean?

The Jewish Sabbath has always been a day given specially to what we should call church-going. To most Jews that has meant worship in the local synagogue. There have been long prayers, some of them very beautiful in their praise of God. There have been psalms, the reading of scripture, and sermons. All this we should expect. How else has the Sabbath been kept holy?

Jewish teachers, the rabbis, have attached a great deal of importance to the order to do no work. They have made list after list of things which might be counted work. (This has come about largely as a result of people's questions.) When Jesus was a boy he was taught that the longest walk allowed on a Sunday was less than a mile, the 'Sabbath day's journey'. A walk longer than that was counted work. To bathe a wound, unless the patient's life was in danger, was also counted work. The Sabbath was made into a day of 'don'ts' and so has remained among orthodox, that is strict, Jews till today. In modern times one rule forbids the use either of a pen or pencil on the Sabbath.

Is this how we are meant to keep Sunday? There have been times when people have thought so, and Sundays have been very dreary, particularly for children. But if readers turn to the passages set *For study* in Mark ii and iii they will see that Jesus thought differently from the rabbis about the keeping of the Sabbath. Of course, Jesus counted it important wherever he was to join with others in the worship of God his Father. It was on the question of other occupations that he and the Jewish leaders disagreed. Have you noticed that on one Sabbath in Capernaum (*a*) Jesus did not go out to his work of preaching and healing, he went to the synagogue; but (*b*) while there he was ready to give teaching (when asked); and (*c*) while there he healed a suffering man, who drew his attention? Have you noticed that (*d*) he spent that afternoon in a friend's house, and while there (*e*) made things happier for the household by curing his host's mother-in-law of fever?

Jesus' Sabbath was a day when he withdrew from ordinary work. It was a day when he joined with others in worshipping God, when he might spend time in the company of his friends, when he was prepared to use his gifts if needed to make people wiser, or well and happy. The Sabbath, he said, was made for man, not man for the Sabbath.

Jesus' teaching, and his actions on the Sabbath, can help us in answering the question, 'How should we spend our Sunday?'

Jesus withdrew from ordinary work. For millions of people today there is no problem here. If they work in a factory or workshop or assist in an office or shop, their duties may end automatically when the business closes down for the week-end. Some people, however, have to make a choice. The shopkeeper has to deal at some time with his accounts and his orders. Should he deal with them on week-nights and on his early-closing day, or should he leave them over till Sunday? A senior official in the Government, a doctor, an architect, a lawyer, all these may have plenty of 'homework'. So may the student who is working for examinations. So may many others, including the schoolboy and the schoolgirl. It is tempting to all of these to give any spare time to pleasure during the week and get down to their books and papers when it is 'nice and quiet' on Sunday. The teaching of Jesus, though, seems to be that as far as possible we should deal with all ordinary work in the six days allotted to it. If on our holy day we can use our particular skill to give help or happiness to someone else, we should do so. The girl who works at a dress-making business should avoid dress-making on Sunday; but if a friend wants help with her cutting-out, the girl should be ready to give it. The boy who works at a cycle-shop may groan when he is asked to mend a punctured tyre for one of his family on a Sunday ('You do it so quickly and easily'), but he should be ready to do it all the same.

Some people, of course, have to work on a Sunday. In the country, as of old, beasts have to be fed, cows to be milked. Now that so many live in cities, certain people are called on to do a regular turn of Sunday duty in connection with public utilities—gas works, electric power stations, water-pumping stations. All over the country, milk distributors go on their rounds. For the work of these people we should be grateful. They make all the difference to our day of rest. There are many other Sunday workers. Which of them are doing work that is really necessary?

Suppose readers at this point jot down on rough paper two lists, one labelled *necessary work* and the other *unnecessary work*. The first will contain probably the items mentioned above—and what else? The second may or may not contain, say, Sunday buses and the printing and distributing of Sunday papers. If lists are compared, it will probably be found that no two persons' are exactly alike. Many of us disagree as to what we expect others to do for us so that we can make what we think is the best of our Sunday.

One person who is commonly expected to do a seven-day week is the mother of a family. Sunday may be her hardest day. This is specially true when the family takes for granted that her business is to cook for them a big Sunday dinner, dish it, serve it, clear away, and wash up. Those at home from shop or factory, office or school, through skilful work at the sink can do much to lighten the mother's Sunday. A boy known to the writer learned as a 'fag' at a public school to be very smart at washing-up. When the household at home was large, he would

Christiana, her sons, and Mercy set out for the Celestial City. Mrs. Timorous stays behind

organize a team of washers-up. They had to work carefully but smartly, singing all the time!

A reader may say, 'I grant you that some mothers have a hard time on Sundays. Many people though, like Sunday work. They get double pay, or at least time and a half, and they get another day off for rest.' That is true, but what the reader implies is that some people see sense in money but not in Sunday. A holy day is meant to be special, not only because it is one of rest from work but because of its connection with God. It is a day on which we are meant to withdraw our attention from the world of the moment, the world of earning and spending, and let ourselves remember the world that lies beyond, the world of everlasting life. Jesus on the Sabbath day went to the synagogue. Sunday worship together is the old, old custom of the Christian Church. Readers of *Servants of God at Work* may remember Justin's description of how on the day of the Sun, some eighteen hundred years ago, Christians from town and country came together. They came to hear the Bible read and explained, to pray together, to share in the sacred meal, the Eucharist or Thanksgiving. They came, too, to bring some contribution towards the help of those of their company who were in need.

To Justin and his friends their church-going mattered so much that they met together at the risk of their lives. Ours should matter to us enough for us to take trouble about it and perhaps risk jibes from companions.

Know ye that the Lord he is God: it is he that made us, and not we ourselves; we are his people, and the sheep of his pasture.

Enter into his gates with thanksgiving, and into his courts with praise; be thankful unto him, and bless his name.

If we believe with the writer of this psalm that we really belong to God's flock, we should be ready to make the necessary effort to go to church or chapel to praise him. There, too, we can tell him of our failures and ask for help for the future.

Sunday then may mean to us, as the Sabbath to Jesus, a day of rest from ordinary work, and a day when we can join with others in worshipping God. As Jesus too, we can make our holy day one when we enjoy the company of our friends. Sunday is even more than a Sabbath, though; it reminds us of the new beginning of things when Christ rose from the dead. It should be a day of recreation (look carefully at that word), a day of refreshment. On Sunday those who have to work indoors may get out of doors, and those people who in the week have no time to read, or to listen to music, or enjoy hobbies, can do so. It is a day for the kind of pleasures which make us feel a new person, not for those which are selfish, or leave the boy or girl, the man or woman, tired, cross, or thick in the head, to face the week's work.

CHAPTER XXI

The first shall be last

For study

Riches are in the way

Mark x. 21, 22

Who is the greatest?

Mark x. 35-37, 41-45

For extra reading

The master is the servant

John xiii. 1-7, 12-14

Blessed are the meek

Matthew v. 5

Psalm xxxvii. 11

WHAT am I to do? That was the question asked at the beginning of this term's work. How am I to make the best of life? How am I, as a young man once put it, 'to gain eternal life'? The answer on page 60 was given from the teaching of Jesus. He advised that young man, if he wanted to enter into life, to begin by keeping the Commandments, those which are concerned with our behaviour to other people.

That was not the end of the story though. The young man was sure that he had kept these Commandments ever since he was a lad. (Maybe he had. He was obviously very serious, very earnest.) Still, he was not satisfied with himself. What else did he need to do? Jesus replied (according to Matthew's version):

If thou wilt be perfect, go and sell that thou hast, and give to the poor, and thou shalt have treasure in heaven: and come and follow me.

There you have it. Jesus knew that all this young man's goodness was cushioned by wealth and position and comfort. Was he ready to have all these cushions tweaked away, all his props removed? Was he prepared to sell his fields and vineyards, his cattle and sheep and goats? Was he prepared to find himself without a single slave to wait on him? Was he ready to hand over all his money to those who were in need? Was he ready to offer his extra education, as well as his health and strength, in God's service? The young man found that Jesus was asking too much. He went away sorrowful.

Jesus then told his disciples, to their astonishment, that a rich man would not enter God's Kingdom easily.

He explained, as St. Mark shows, that it is difficult to enter God's Kingdom while you are banking on any kind of riches, money or land, or even the love and care you get from father or mother, wife or children. A person who wants to enter God's Kingdom must be prepared to give up everything of his own if he is asked. (Some people say that God is asking what is humanly impossible. Yet they know that thousands of people have, of their own free will, given up happy, comfortable homes and good jobs to fight and die for their country.)

The young man was from the point of view of Jesus' teaching very much a beginner. You notice that his concern was for himself. He did not ask, What must I do to serve God? Jesus began to use the word 'serve' in a way which Jews were not accustomed to. Servants to them were mostly slaves, people who were not encouraged to have a mind of their own. Of course Jews knew that to serve might be considered a noble thing. Moses was called 'the servant of the Lord'. The prophet Elisha as a young man followed Elijah as his servant. He dedicated himself to the service of this great man. He was at the same time his disciple, his pupil. All Jews knew too the story of the young King Rehoboam, told in I Kings xii. His experienced advisers warned him that if he wanted the support of his people he must be prepared to be their servant and help them in their troubles instead of putting burdens on them. Rehoboam preferred to listen to proud, ignorant young men. When he addressed his people he insisted on talking as if he meant to be a bully and a dictator, and he suffered for it. So he should, all good Jews would think. Their proverb says,

> Pride goeth before destruction, and a haughty spirit before a fall.

Still the Jews, Jesus' followers included, took it as natural that most people should want to get to the top. It seemed natural, too, that at the top you should be the person who gives orders, the person on whom other people wait.

Now read the passages from Mark x set *For study*. Jesus says clearly there that among his followers the person at the top is the one who makes it his business to serve others, the person who is ready to take the lowest position. He himself came to serve.

Jesus illustrated the same point by his own actions on the night before he suffered. St. John tells how he, the master of the feast, rose from the supper table. Taking a towel and a basin of water, he went to each of his disciples and knelt to wash their feet—just as if he were a slave. To Peter, who was puzzled and disturbed, he explained that this was what the disciples should do for one another.

Here then is Christ's commandment: 'Whoever wants to be great among you must be your servant'. (Mark x. 44, in a modern version.) Put in another way, If you want to live to the full, you must serve.

How does this commandment work out for ourselves? For many boys and girls the commandment means readiness to help at home, not just to be waited on by the mother of the household from the first cup of tea to the clearing away of the last supper plate. It may mean giving up your own pleasures because you are needed at home. For those at school, to follow Christ's teaching means to put your best into everything you do in class, even if you never 'shine' at anything. It means being ready to accept dull duties and to do them cheerfully. It means in a dramatic club being ready to take small parts, even if you feel that you could fairly be asked to do something bigger, or in a sports club not slacking because you fail to be chosen for a team. It means preparing yourself for work in which you can be of service to other people.

A boy known to the writer determined to train as a chef. He was a public-school boy, and some people were surprised. Why spend hot hours in a kitchen? Why not choose a white-collar job? When the boy had finished his training he was so skilled that he got offers of jobs in more than one expensive restaurant. The wages were big. Perhaps that was what he hoped for? or perhaps he had the ambition to be a famous chef in one of these restaurants? No. He refused these jobs. He had always meant, he said, to be a cook in a hospital. The pay might not be nearly so much. He might not have such exciting things to cook. He might have to spend a great deal of his time cooking 'standard diets', food for the people in the hospital who had nothing wrong with their digestion. The young man knew, though, how much it matters that people in hospital should have their food properly cooked. He knew, too, that skilled cooks are needed if people with certain kinds of illness are to have the food which will help them to recover. So into a big hospital the young man went, as a junior cook. It was a place where he would be serving sick people, though they would never see him, never know all that they owed to his work.

As a junior cook the young man had to serve not only the patients but those above him in the kitchens. He must cook what and when he was ordered. He is a clever chef, though, and a hard worker. The time comes for such a young man when he gets the chance to be

Christiana, Mercy, and the boys are led up the hill Difficulty by Mr. Great-Heart

head cook, perhaps, of some great hospital. Then a new test comes. Does he see himself as the servant not only of his patients but of his big kitchen staff? If so, he will be their friend. Or does he count power as more important than service, and become a 'big boss'? Christ's teaching is clear. His servants are here not to be ministered unto but to minister, whatever position they occupy in the outside world.

Blessed are the meek: for they shall inherit the earth.

Jesus once said these words. He did not mean, as some people seem to think, 'Blessed are the namby-pamby', but rather 'Blessed are those who don't set themselves up'. A person who determines to serve God and other people has a line to work on and all the scope he wants. There are opportunities for him on every side. The world is his. The person who sets out to fight for his own hand, to be top-dog, may grasp at a lot and get something. The world is never his.

PART THREE

Puzzles and Paradoxes

by

Catherine B. Firth

INTRODUCTION TO PART THREE

(for those readers only who like puzzling)

THIS Part is different from all the other Parts in the four books of *Roads to Christian Faith*. The chapters are planned in answer to questions asked towards the end of their secondary school life by boys and girls in different parts of Britain. The chapters do not follow one from another. They may be read in any order.

The principal question with which each chapter deals is printed at its beginning. Readers may find that different questions which they have thought of come into one or another chapter. The principal questions are the Puzzles mentioned in the title *Puzzles and Paradoxes*.

Paradoxes are expressed in sentences which have two parts, each seeming to contradict the other. 'Para' means 'alongside' (as in the word 'parallel', used in *Roads of Israel*, pp. 48, 49); it may also have the meaning 'alongside, and different'. 'Dox' means an opinion. In a paradox two different opinions or ideas are laid alongside, and it looks at first sight as though both could not be true. The first paradox which puzzled the writer was one she found, as a child, in an old-fashioned book. It said: 'Mary Jane was a nice girl, but she was cross and told lies'.

Towards the end of each chapter in this Part there is usually a paradox which has something to do with the puzzle printed at the chapter's beginning. Paradoxes (like the one about Mary Jane) may be puzzling; but (*paradoxically*) many puzzles can only be solved by paradoxes.

CHAPTER XXII

The puzzle of independence

For study

Christians do not live separately
Romans xii. 3-5; xiv. 7, 8

The example of the Good Shepherd
John x. 11-18

For extra reading

Belonging to each other
1 Corinthians xii. 13-27

Can't I do what I like?

MOST boys and girls who read this Part of *The End of the Roads* will soon be schoolboys and schoolgirls no longer. They will have cleared out their desks and tidied their books and tools for the last time. Leaving schooldays behind, they will have passed through the gates into the world of men and women.

Probably most boys and girls will, somewhere, feel a twinge of regret. Certainly the majority will be more glad than sorry. The world is big; there is so much to do and see. People with courage and energy intend to live their own lives and to make the best of them. They want to be independent and free.

Here readers may find it interesting to stop reading for two minutes by the clock and jot down on rough paper as many ways as they can think of in which grown-up life is more independent than school life. If there is time in the two minutes, they might go through the lists and put question-marks against any points which may on second thoughts seem doubtful.

A point which will probably have been written on most lists is that the end of school life means the end of the need to obey school rules and follow school customs. School rules and customs, Yes. But all rules and customs? Some readers may wonder about a question mark there, thinking, 'Grown-up life is not really free from things like that'. They know that a home without its own rules and customs would be rather like an animal's cage in the Zoo. Even boys and girls who hate having to come in punctually to meals know, when they stop to think, that they would be indignant if their mother said it was too hard for her to get breakfast and dinner and tea at the proper times. Every reader will be able to remember other ways in which the independence of each member of a household, grown-up or child, is limited.

'Yes', someone may say, 'but grown-up people do what they want much oftener than boys and girls. I know I am not quite grown-up when I leave school, but I soon shall be, and I ought to be treated as though I were. I shall be earning, and I intend to get a job that I like.'

Sensible remarks of that kind lead on to another point which may have a place on the list written in those two minutes. While a boy is at school—or a girl, of course—he depends on his parents or guardians for his housing and food, his holidays, his pocket-money, his way of living in general. His father earns for the family and, within limits, can choose his job; if he dislikes the work, the pay, or the employer, he can leave. Naturally, no sensible boy (or girl) expects to earn an adult's wage when he first begins, but as soon as he can pay something towards his keep, buy his own extras, take his girl friend to the pictures, and so on, he feels well on the way to grown-up independence.

But again, is that kind of independence as great as it looks? The father, perhaps, learned a trade he comes later to hate. He cannot change without loss of money, for he will have to begin again at the bottom; and he cannot afford loss of money, because he now has a wife and family to provide for. Or the factory he has worked in closes down and he loses the job he likes. Or his trade union considers a strike; he may vote against it, but if the majority of members are in favour he too will be obliged to come out. The mother, perhaps, as a girl had some special amusement she liked, but now she has to look after the children and maybe earn for them as well; anyhow, she may get too tired, for she must be up early to prepare sandwiches or cook the breakfast. Partly through conditions of work; partly through responsibilities for other people; partly, perhaps, through bad health—grown-up people's power to choose is, in one way or another, much less complete than it looks.

The first answer to the question at the head of this chapter is easy. 'Can't I do what I like?' 'No; life doesn't work that way.' No-one is quite independent. Whether we like it or not, all of us are mixed up with each other.

Of course, in some ways we do like it. Hardly anybody, man or woman, boy or girl, wants to live quite alone. Most men and women, like boys and girls, need to do things and share things with other people. But as soon as you say that, you have really said that hardly anybody wants to be quite independent. What most of us mean if we say that we do is simply, 'I want my own way all the time'. And that—as everyone who has played team games or carried out any ploy with a friend knows perfectly well—is impossible.

There is another reason why doing what one likes does not, on second thoughts, look so attractive as at first sight it often appears. A boy (or girl)who had to be almost 'quite independent' when he left school would not just be lonely. Very soon he would find the choices in front of him hard to make. He would feel as a man who rows well on a river would feel if he found himself on the open sea alone in a high-powered motor launch. If he makes bad choices there is no-one to warn him. A bad choice of action at sea might bring its own punishment quickly enough, but in life the bad results of bad choices may not show for years and years. At school, however independent boys and girls in the top classes are expected to be, there is someone to warn against dangers, and in some schools at least the penalty for mistakes or wrong-doing comes quickly! At the time, that is unpleasant; but it is better than finding out too late that a bad habit—begun, perhaps, in ignorance—is bringing results one never thought of.

Or take religion. At school, there are prayers every day. There are Scripture lessons. There are people round, teachers or pupils, who want to be good. Many boys and girls may feel they will be glad to be free of all that kind of thing, some because they don't want to serve God, and probably a number more because they think they can serve him quite well on their own. When they are out in the world, work or pleasures may pull the other way. Or, as they get older, they may find their ideas about God are still childish, and jump to the childish conclusion that that is God's fault. In their wish to be independent, they may have cut themselves off from the people and places where they could have learnt to grow up in religion.

The first answer to the question at the head of the chapter was 'No'. The second answer is another question: 'Are you perfectly sure you want to be quite independent?' To that question, in spite of what the last few pages have said, many boys and girls would still answer, 'Yes—at least, perhaps not quite, but nearly'.

To want to be independent is good. The amount of

freedom it is useful for boys and girls to have when they first leave school depends upon them and their circumstances. No-one who is sensible will try to manage without any help or advice, and no-one in Britain need. If a boy or girl does not want to ask for either at home he can go to an employer or foreman; to a minister; to a citizens' advice bureau, or to the police. (One difference between the times before and after leaving school is this. In school, teachers do not wait for pupils to ask to be taught; afterwards, the older people most able to help often hold back until those who are younger come to them.)

In a very few years the people who are reading this book will be men and women, and then, they feel, the time will have come to be really independent. So it will. Men and women should not be jelly-fish—creatures without a backbone, and neither should they be sheep, ready to follow in a mass, maybe pushing each other and with no clear notion of where they are going.

It would be interesting to stop at this point and ask how many readers noticed that the last time the word 'independent' was used the word before it was different from the word before 'independent' printed earlier in this chapter. If any reader did not notice, perhaps he will look again at pages 182, 183.

Being really independent is different from being quite independent. In fact, it is the opposite. A hockey player may see the ball coming to him and long to run it up the field himself. But he knows his place in the game. Shall he pass out to the wing? or dribble for a moment till centre-half is ready? Or send to the right to frustrate the plan of the other team? He must choose. In a second he must decide and act. He has much more

Teach me, my God and King,
In all things Thee to see,
And what I do in anything,
To do it as for Thee.

A servant with this clause
Makes drudgery divine:
Who sweeps a room as for Thy laws,
Makes that and th'action fine.

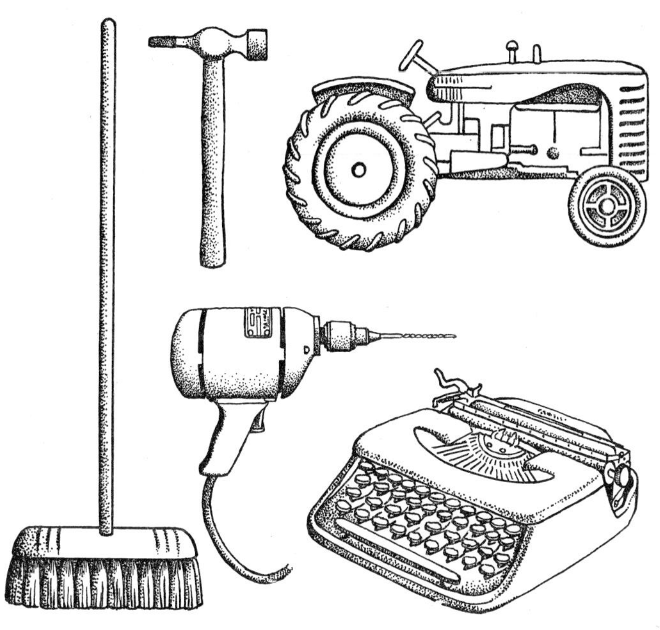

'What I do in anything'

real independence—independence which counts—than if he was quite independent, knocking a ball about just for his own amusement. Or take another example. The young man and woman who decide to marry and make a home are becoming dependent each of them on the other, but neither is troubled by the thought of not doing what he or she likes all the time.

Real independence comes when people are able to let their 'quite independence' go for the sake of something they choose because they think it is more important. The hockey player gives up the independence of play for himself; he is independent because he chooses to play for the team. The young man and woman give up independence because they have chosen each other.

The most independent man who ever lived is Jesus, who chose to do God's will. The next most independent people are men and women who have chosen to try to live as he lived.

Jesus died on the cross, nailed there by Roman soldiers. Yet he said that no-one took his life from him; he himself laid it down. 'I have power to lay it down,' he said, 'and I have power to take it again.' And he gave the reason. He said that he was doing what God, his Father, had told him. Jesus was perfectly independent because he always wanted to do, and did, what God wanted him to do.

Men and women who have tried to follow Jesus have been independent too. They, too, have wanted to do the will of God more than to have their own way. So they have been able to stand up for what they knew was right even when they were laughed at. They have often chosen to do things for other people when they longed to do something else. They have been willing to die when they thought God was asking them for that. All such Christians have proved that there was no need to be afraid of painful things or dull things or bad things, because they depended on God. So they were really independent.

Readers who use the Prayer Book may know a prayer which speaks of real independence. It comes in the service called Morning Prayer.

O God . . . whose service is perfect freedom; Defend us thy humble servants in all assaults [attacks] of our enemies; that we, surely trusting in thy defence, may not fear the power of any adversaries, through the might of Jesus Christ our Lord.

CHAPTER XXIII

The puzzle of difference

For study

The world (a)

John iii. 16, 17

The world (b)

1 John ii. 15-17

Separate—from what?

2 Corinthians vi. 16-18

For extra reading

A prayer for Christians in (a)

John xvii. 6-18, 25, 26

Christians are different

1 John iv. 4-11

The need for self-control

Matthew xviii. 8, 9

Must Christians be different?

THAT depends on what sort of difference you mean. Christians worship the God whom Jesus, both by what he taught and by what he did, explained to men. Christians try to be as much like Jesus in character as they can. They try to do what they think he wishes them to do. They know that they are only able even to try to follow him if he helps them. They own up when they fail. They know that God will accept an honest apology, and they fight on (look again at page 96).

People who are not Christians do not believe what Christians believe about Jesus, nor do they usually aim at doing all that Christians try to do; for example, some of them think that it is weak to say they are sorry when they have done wrong, or to forgive people who have done wrong to them.

This does not mean that non-Christians may not often seem to be nicer than Christians. The point here is not what any reader thinks about that; it is simply that Christians and non-Christians agree that they are different from each other. They know that they think and feel differently about God, and about how they want to behave towards him and often towards people.

It was not that kind of difference which the girl who asked the question at the head of this chapter had in her mind. She was not thinking about the kind of subject discussed in Parts One and Two of this book, but about smaller matters of conduct on which Christians do not all agree. This is what she wrote:

When a young girl is growing up she naturally wishes to attend dancing and possibly the cinema. My Sunday School teacher understood when I told her that I still liked the cinema, but she added that most Christians feel out of place in such a place.

That girl had not been a Christian long, but the question she asked has been a puzzle for hundreds of years. Since the Church began Christians have asked: Ought we to be different? Does God want us to separate ourselves from our non-Christian friends? Are ordinary amusements 'worldly'? And what does 'worldly' mean?

Christians who want to know what they ought to do naturally think that the answer must be in the Bible. But there are no rules in the Bible about dancing and cinemas or the other amusements which modern people enjoy. There are no Christian rules such as: You must not attend dances; you must not go to the pictures; you must not turn on television. If there were rules like that, the answer to the question would in one way be easy: if these things are forbidden for Christians, then Christians must certainly be different. In another way, if detailed rules of that kind had been made for Christians by the writers of the New Testament, they would not be of much use now. None of the amusements which depend on the discoveries of modern science had then been invented; any detailed list written, for example, by Paul would have been out of date long ago.

There is still another, more important, reason why there are no rules of that kind in the New Testament. The writers wanted people to think for themselves, as Jesus had shown he too wanted. Jesus and the first Christian teachers gave men and women big ideas—

principles—and left them to work out the details for their own lives themselves.

Jesus did not say that his disciples ought not to spend their free time in this way or that. He said:

> If thy eye is an occasion of falling to thee [makes you do wrong], pluck it out and cast [throw] it away from thee; better for thee to enter into life with one eye, than to have two eyes when thou art cast into the fires of hell.

Here Jesus was using picture-language as he so often did. He meant that it is better for a man to give up anything he has, however precious, than to let it separate him from God.

The writers of the Epistles did not lay down the rule that Christians must keep away from places like the stadium at Corinth or the huge theatre at Ephesus. When Paul wrote, 'Come out from among them and be ye separate', he was thinking—so it seems from the sentences round that one—of the whole heathen life of the time, with its worship of idols and wickedness. All the same, he and other writers had a great deal to say about the question at the head of this chapter.

The word 'worldly' comes straight out of verses in the New Testament. (Some of them are set *For study* and *For extra reading*.) It means, of course, belonging to the world. That sounds easy. But 'world' in the New Testament has two different meanings, one big (*a*), one smaller (*b*).

The big meaning (*a*) is that the world is all that God has made, including the most important things—men and women (though 'things' is not usually the right word for people!). It includes, too, good things which men and women have made. World is used in that

Two meanings of 'world'
Which things are often in 'b'?

sense in John iii. 16, a verse set *For Study* which readers should look at now.

The smaller meaning (*b*) is that the world is all the things in (*a*) which might be used for God and instead often keep men and women away from him. The word is used in that sense in 1 John ii. 15 (read the verse now).

The word 'worldly' means belonging to the world in the (*b*) sense. Worldly people may call themselves Christians, but they do not feel that God matters more than anything else. They behave as if getting money, or amusing themselves, or dressing well, was more important than God. It is not wrong to earn money or to have ordinary fun or to look nice. Christians who are not worldly often do all these things, that is, they live in (*a*) as people do who are not Christians; in that sense, they are not 'different'. But people who make money, or pleasure, or their looks, more important than God are 'worldly': they live in (*b*) as well as (*a*). In that sense real Christians must be 'different'.

Jesus once prayed for his disciples and for all future Christians in words which show in what sense he wanted them to be different from other people. He said to God:

> I am not asking that thou shouldst take them out of the world, but that thou shouldst keep them clear of what is evil.

(That is a modern translation; the English words in the Authorized Version are not quite the same.)

In that prayer Jesus used 'world' in the (*a*) meaning. In the second part of the prayer 'what is evil' means much the same as world in the (*b*) meaning: the expression includes what is bad in itself and also what is used badly. None of the little pictures on page 192 show things bad in themselves, but some are of things which are often used badly. All the things belong to (*a*); some are often found in (*b*).

One of the easiest ways of being worldly is in amusements. That was what puzzled the girl who asked the question about dancing and cinemas. She meant, Should Christians have different pleasures from other people?

Of course no Christian ought to join in amusements which are cruel or unkind or in themselves bad in other ways. Torturing an animal; frightening small children; laughing at people because they are old or ugly or lame; getting drunk; behaving or persuading companions to behave in ways you would be ashamed to be found out in by people you respect: such amusements are certainly unfit for Christians. The puzzle comes not about them but about things which some Christians think bad in themselves and some think good.

Here it will be useful to compare different classes of amusement with different kinds of fruit. Some berries are poisonous: no-one who is sensible will eat the fruit of deadly nightshade or bryony, however attractive it may look. Such fruits are like amusements which are bad in themselves. Secondly, some fruits—apples for example—are thought by everyone to be good to eat, though some people like them more than others do. Such fruits may be compared with team games and sports. Thirdly, there are fruits which are not poisonous but give some people indigestion. Black currants, for example, make some people quite ill. These fruits are like the puzzling amusements, good for many people but not for everyone. We are not all made alike.

There is also another way in which fruit may be compared with amusements. Children are told what they may or may not eat. Grown-up people can remember what they were taught as children, but they must decide, and often find out, for themselves.

Boys and girls who are Christians may discover that some amusements make it harder for them to serve God, even though their companions seem to take no harm. Dancing may excite some people so much that they go on to behave in ways they would not really choose: for example, they may drink too much, or get silly with each other. The pictures may fill a girl's head with day-dreams, or a boy's with second-rate ambitions. Any amusement may encourage a boy or girl to spend more time or money on it than he or she can afford.

In such ways as these pleasures not bad in themselves are like black currants—bad for some people. Any young man or woman who discovers that some amusement gives him or her 'indigestion' is either foolish or weak (or both!) if he does not try to pull up quickly, even if that means making new friends. If he does not, he may lose his independence. Before long he may find himself unable to stop; the pleasure may be ordering him about.

Some Christians find it helpful in learning self-control to make a private rule for a fixed time. He or she may decide that he will not go to dances in Lent (the six weeks before Easter); or that he will only go to a cinema so many times in the next month; or that for so long he will not spend more on his pet pleasure than a certain sum. After he has kept his rule for the time he has planned, he will probably be independent enough of a pleasure to look at it all round. He will be able to decide for himself, instead of being led by companions, or pushed about by his own excitement or changing moods. He will have had time, too, to remember that what he does may be important for other people: there are always younger or weaker boys and girls who will follow someone they admire.

A pleasure in which both self-control and example are of special importance is gambling. To some people, gambling is like poisonous fruit: no Christian, they think, should touch it. Other people see it as belonging to the black currant class: to take a chance of gain and be prepared to lose, is not, they think, unchristian in itself. They would call a person who takes too many chances not so much wicked as silly: each time he risks even sixpence, he is, in fact, more likely to lose that useful sum than to win more money—it is 'a mug's game'.

Whether people think that gambling is unchristian or that it is wrong only when badly used, everyone agrees that once it has become a habit gambling is hard to stop. It may lead people to risk more than they can afford, or even money which is not really theirs: 'better luck next time' they say, and take another chance. At last it may not even be a pleasure; it may become a sort of excited demon, driving a man beyond his own will. Many Christian boys and girls will perhaps decide that they will not begin; if so, by their own choice they will be 'different'.

It is not easy to belong to (*a*) and not to (*b*). God leaves to those who serve him so much choice over details that they often agree with the poet Robert Browning who wrote:

> How very hard it is to be
> A Christian! . . .
> And where we looked for crowns to fall,
> We find the tug's to come,—that's all.

An old prayer asks God himself to make men and women want to be different in the ways which he wants for them. (Readers who use the Prayer Book will find that it is the Collect for the fourth Sunday after Easter.)

O almighty God, who alone canst order the unruly wills and affections of sinful men; Grant unto thy people, that they may love the thing which thou commandest, and desire that which thou dost promise; that so, among the sundry and manifold [the various and many] changes of the world, our hearts may surely there be fixed, where true joys are to be found.

CHAPTER XXIV

The puzzle of fairness

For study

The parable of the talents
Matthew xxv. 14-30

or

The parable of the pounds
Luke xix. 11-27

A reading for the end of the chapter
Proverbs iii. 5, 6, 26

For extra reading

The parable of the labourers in the vineyard
Matthew xx. 1-16

Why didn't God make us all good?

THERE was once a headmaster of a big school who was very strict. The boys—when he wasn't about—called him a beast. All the same, they respected and liked him. 'He's a beast,' they said, 'but a just beast.'

The laws of a well-governed country have to be fair, and fairly enforced. Even that is not enough: they have to be expressed, and used in the law courts, in such a way that people can see they are fair.

Schools and countries and homes too are unhappy where there are favourites. Even if people think that favouritism is possible, they quickly grumble: 'It isn't fair'. Readers might stop here, and try to remember what had happened the last time they made, or heard, that remark.

Good teachers and rulers and parents do their best to be fair. It is all the more strange, then, that God so often seems to be unfair.

'It's easy for X to be good: he hasn't got my bad temper.' 'Of course Y behaves well at home: she positively enjoys washing up and dusting.' 'Z never gets into trouble for bad manners at meals—he doesn't *want* to be greedy', or, 'he says he *likes* fish!' 'I'm always being scolded: it isn't fair.'

'X can do eight sums to my three, and I work just as hard.' 'Y reads the poetry through twice and knows it; I say it over and over and in the end make mistakes.' 'Z is always being told he does straight, clean work: my carpentry—or cooking—or sewing—goes wrong, though

I try and try.' 'Why should So-and-so get all the praise? I can't help being myself. It isn't fair.'

'X can sing, or paint, or act.' 'Y has curly hair, lovely blue eyes, a good complexion.' 'Z always wins in the high jump, or swimming, or the 50-yards flat race. He is good at it. I'm not. It isn't fair.'

Things are no better if someone says: 'Of course he can run: his father played for the county'; or, 'It would be odd if she wasn't good-looking, her mother was the prettiest girl in the town'. 'Why shouldn't *my* father have been an athlete?' 'Why wasn't *I* the daughter of a beautiful woman?' Why didn't God let us all be born with the gifts we most admire? It isn't fair.

Or take circumstances. 'Why can A and B have the tools or the clothes or the holidays they want because their parents are rich, and I can't?' 'Why do C and D come from happy homes while E and F are not properly cared for? Why is G going on to learn the trade he likes best, when J is obliged to take the first job that comes?' Why hasn't God given us all the same chances of getting on? It isn't fair.

Many boys and girls would not feel it right to grumble about God in that way. Yet that is what they are doing if they believe that he is real and go on complaining about the things they did not decide for themselves—what they start with (their heredity) or the circumstances of their lives (their environment). 'Why didn't God make us all good, or clever, or rich? Why couldn't he have let everyone start fair?'

The puzzle of fairness is there all the time. No-one has solved it completely. All the same, there are things to say, some known through experience and common sense, some known straight from the Bible.

(1) *What common sense says*

(*a*) Fairness is not the same as equality. Of course, if there are eight children of about the same age at a party and there is only one cake, 'fair shares' means a slice all round, of equal size, with an equal amount of sugar-icing. But if the eight children were of one family, the eldest fifteen and the youngest under a year, no-one would think it fair to divide the cake into eight equal parts, one for each child. At once it is clear that fairness, even about a thing which can be cut into equal divisions, is not so simple as that: the people who are to have the shares have to be thought of as well as the thing.

(*b*) Things are not always so unfair as they look. The clever boy may come from an unhappy home. The boy who is a good swimmer may never be near the top of his class. The girl who is stupid at arithmetic may be excellent at taking care of babies. Everyone has something he is good at, or something he specially enjoys. A boy of nine who was injured in a road accident found as he got better that he could not do well at school, but he was happy and proud when he discovered he could lift heavier weights than other boys of his age.

No-one really knows enough about other people's lives to make comparisons between the lives as if they were so many bricks of fixed size. No-one really knows if he is happier or better off—except in the most outside sense—than someone else. As the old proverb puts it, 'Only the wearer knows where the shoe pinches'.

(*c*) Men and women cannot really make everything fair for each other, however much they try. Imagine that everyone who left a certain school at the same time was given ten pounds to do what he or she liked with, and had no other pocket-money: would they all be equally rich at the end of a month? Of course not, though people would say they had 'started fair'. Or think of two children with the same parents, and the same upbringing: would you expect them to have the same characters and the same successes?

Common sense shows that the puzzle of fairness is different from what it seems to be. For that reason, common sense may help people to be less impatient about unfairness. But it does not solve the puzzle.

(2) *What the Bible says*

Christians who read the New Testament have more to say than has common sense by itself. Jesus told three parables which have something to do with the puzzle of fairness. Two of them are about rewards.

(i) *The parable of the talents.* Readers will probably remember this story. It is found in Matthew xxv. 14-30, one of the alternative sets of verses set *For study*. A man who was going on a long journey entrusted different sums of money—five talents or two, or one—to each of three servants, so that they might use the money to earn more for him by the time he came back. (A talent was a certain weight of silver.) Two servants traded faithfully and each managed to double the sum he had received. The third dug a hole in the ground and hid the talent which the master had trusted him with. Any reader who has forgotten what happened when the master came home can find out by reading the verses set.

In this parable there are four points to notice.

First, the man who has received most—the man with special gifts—has bigger responsibilities. More is expected of him.

Secondly, the two men who have worked well receive exactly the same praise. Each has done his best with what he has received. The man who was given less pleases the master as much as the man who began with more.

Thirdly, the wicked, lazy servant is scolded and punished. He was not, in the ordinary sense, a thief—he did not steal the money. But he had not tried to use it, partly because he was lazy; partly, perhaps, because he was cross and jealous over being given a smaller sum than the other servants. When he knows that he will not be trusted again, and is dismissed his master's service, he really has nothing to grumble about. So far the servant might have thought the master 'a beast, but a just beast'.

The last point to notice is in Matthew xxv. 29. Every reader should look at that verse, and see if he thinks that what it says is fair.

(ii) *The parable of the pounds*. This is told in Luke xix. 12-27. Anyone who wishes can read that story instead of the parable of the talents.

In the parable of the pounds, each servant is given the same sum of money to trade with (a pound, like a talent, is a certain weight of silver, but smaller). Two of them earn different sums. Each receives the same praise, and a reward in proportion to—what? (There is no suggestion in the story that anyone thought that unfair.) In both stories, too, there is one servant who has done nothing useful with what was entrusted to him. In both, what he has is taken away, and is given to the man whose trading has earned most. Here, the ending is remarked on by men who stood by (whether those who were listening to Jesus, or the bystanders in the story is not clear). They exclaimed, as any of us might have done, 'But he has got ten pounds! It isn't fair.' Then St. Luke quotes just the same saying of Jesus as St. Matthew quotes at the end of the parable of the talents.

Jesus, clearly, did not think that either the best or the worst of the servants in the story of the pounds was being unfairly treated. It was not unfair that the man who did not use what had been given to him should lose it. It was not unfair that the man who had worked hardest should have a special reward. That is what happens in the world God has made. A good singing voice, or strong muscles, will become weak if they are not used. A good mind, the power to make friends, even a man's love of God, is developed with exercise.

(iii) *The parable of the labourers in the vineyard.* This story tells of an employer who at the beginning of a day agreed with workmen on a certain wage. Later in the day, others came to work for him, even down to within an hour of leaving off for the night. You shall be paid what is right, he said. In the evening, the employer handed the wages to his steward who paid them out as he had been told. The men then discovered that each of them had been given the pay—the 'penny'—which had been accepted by those who by evening had worked through the long, hot day. That group felt they had a grievance. Angrily they said to the employer, 'You can't treat those others the same as us! It isn't fair.' The owner of the vineyard answered: 'I have given you what you agreed on. As to the others, it is for me to decide. Why should you be mean because I am generous?'

This parable has probably more than one meaning. One of the points which Jesus meant to make was, I

And I said to the man who stood at the gate of the year: 'Give me a light that I may tread safely into the unknown.'

And he replied:

'Go out into the darkness and put your hand into the Hand of God. That shall be to you better than light and safer than a known way.'

A page to illustrate Proverbs iii. 6

think, that many things which God gives to people are not rewards at all, but just presents.

The most important gift which God offers to men and women is what the Bible calls eternal life—the life which is a sharing of his own life. That is something too great for anyone to earn. Paul says so clearly:

> The wages of sin [wages are earned] is death; but the gift of God is eternal life through Jesus Christ our Lord.

That gift is the same for every one who wants it. It is like and yet unlike the 'penny' in the parable: like, because it is the same for all; unlike, because it is not a reward for work. No-one deserves eternal life; the question of fairness does not come in.

There are other presents which are not the same for everyone. Those good things about which God seems to be unfair—your special skill at work or games, your good home or good looks, if you have such gifts—were not earned or chosen by you. It was for him to decide. Why should we be mean if he seems to have been specially generous to someone else? We don't know his reasons.

Both common sense and the Bible give help on the puzzle of fairness. Neither solves it completely. After all, the wisest man or woman cannot understand all that God does. His justice is something much bigger than the sharing out of equal bits of cake, or than what we may think is fair. As the prophet Isaiah of Babylon says:

> My thoughts are not your thoughts . . . saith the Lord. For as the heavens are higher than the earth, so are my ways than your ways, and my thoughts than your thoughts.

Some of God's thoughts the Bible does explain. One of these gives a part answer to the question at the head of the chapter. If God had made us all good to start with we should not have been good by our own choice. We should have been good like, say, a well-designed, well-made bicycle, not people with wills of our own. Readers will remember that the story of the Garden of Eden, as well as the Law and the Prophets, shows that God gave men and women the responsibility of choosing between good and evil.

Yet here again comes the puzzle of fairness. God leaves us to choose; but without his help we cannot choose good. Then what about the people who have not learnt about God as Jesus showed that he is? What about children who have bad homes? Why do some people have more chance of choosing good than others?

Paul, like us, knew the puzzle, and he could not solve it. But he was quite sure that no-one is outside the love of God. He was sure, too, that it matters very much what each person does, whatever his or her powers and circumstances; and he was sure that all the time it is God himself who carries out his good plan by making us want to do, and able to do, as he wishes. Paul wrote this paradox:

> Work out your own salvation with fear and trembling [with a sense of responsibility]; for it is God which worketh in you both to will and to do of his good pleasure.

CHAPTER XXV

The puzzle of church-going

For study

'The assembling of ourselves together'

Hebrews x. 23-25

Prayer together

Matthew xviii. 19, 20

Dwelling places of God

Isaiah lvii. 15

For extra reading

An Old Testament story about prayer together

2 Chronicles xx. 1-30

(In verse 14, leave out the words between 'Jahaziel' and 'came')

Does it matter about going to church?

SOME people like going to church. Others do not. To whichever group the reader belongs (most likely the second), it will be useful to write down on a rough piece of paper two lists of points about church-going, one for and one against. The lists need be shown to no-one, and can be destroyed when the chapter is finished. Until then they should be kept at hand, ready for ticking if any of the points are the same in the book and the lists.

The New Testament says very little about going to church. The most obvious reason is that there were no churches to go to. The earliest Christians could only 'go to church' in a house. Paul preached to Christians in an upstairs room in Troas. The slave Onesimus perhaps had to prepare the room for the meetings of Christians held in the house of Philemon, his master, in Colossae.

Such little meetings were counted very important. There Christians listened to teaching, and talked with each other, about Jesus. There they prayed together, and 'broke bread' as he had commanded. But by the time the Epistle to the Hebrews was written, probably less than forty years after the Day of Pentecost, some Christians did not like going to these meetings. The writer says that they ought not to stay away: if they do, they will lose the chance of backing each other up. His opinion can be read in the first group of verses set *For study*. ('To provoke' is 'to urge' or 'to poke up'; 'exhorting' is 'earnestly advising'.)

Perhaps some of those who forsook 'the assembling of [themselves] together'—gave up going to church—were afraid of persecution from non-Christian Jews. Others, perhaps, felt 'superior': they had been well taught; why should they meet with newly baptized Christians? Or, perhaps, Christian Jews despised these little meetings because they were so different from the solemn ceremonies of the Temple services to which they were accustomed.

Nearly all the earliest Christians, as readers know, were Jews, and the men had been trained as boys to meet with others for the worship of God in synagogues and the Temple. Jews took for granted that this was part of their duty. How, then, did new customs grow up? At first Christian Jews went on worshipping with those who had not been baptized. After Pentecost, Peter and John used to go to the Temple to pray. Paul made plans to get back from his missionary journeys to Jerusalem in time for the Feast of Passover. The idea that a man could be religious all alone, so to speak, would have seemed silly to Jews.

The custom by which Christians and non-Christian Jews joined in the old services did not last long, for two reasons. (1) Quite soon, non-Christians began to persecute Christians: readers will remember how Stephen died. (2) Christians came to see that they could not join in the animal sacrifices offered in the Temple, even at the Passover. Jesus—the Lamb of God—had died to take away the sin of the world. There could be no more need to offer to God 'the blood of goats and of calves', as the writer of Hebrews says. (Animal sacrifices came to an end for non-Christian Jews too when the Temple was destroyed in A.D. 70.)

Gentile Christians, naturally, were not accustomed to Jewish services. All Christians, Jews and Gentiles alike, remembered that Jesus himself had promised to be with 'two or three' of his followers who met together in his name. So the custom of 'going to church' in houses grew. (The second group of verses *For study* should now be read.)

Attendance at little meetings or services on Sunday mornings, especially for the Eucharist (Holy Communion), came to be known as a sign of being a Christian. Justin, the martyr who died about a hundred years later than Paul, wrote of this custom when he was describing what Christians believed and did (*Servants of God at Work*, Chapter XXI). But so long as the Roman government was suspicious of Christians, places where services were held might have to be kept secret.

From the time of Constantine, the first Roman emperor who became Christian (he died in A.D. 337), special buildings for worship—churches—were often put up. Then 'going to church' came to have the outside meaning it has now. The inside meaning has never changed. Christians go to church to worship God together by saying prayers of thanksgiving and asking; by singing psalms and hymns in his praise; by trying to learn more about him from listening to Bible reading and sermons; very specially by carrying out the command of Jesus in the service of Holy Communion. Through nineteen hundred years this kind of Christian worship has gone on. Through nineteen hundred years some people have liked 'going to church', while some have not—and the reasons which the second group give for not going have really been much the same.

Think first about the three reasons which, perhaps, made the Christians spoken of in Hebrews x give up going to church.

(i) *Fear of persecution.* For early Christians, persecution might mean torture and death. So it has done in some lands in modern times. In Britain, we have not been put to that test. But people who go regularly to church may find themselves looked down on as smug or 'sissy'; sneered at or jeered at by their gang; smiled at in an annoying fashion by others whom they would like to have as friends. That kind of persecution in little ways is hard to bear.

All the same, a saying in Proverbs xxiv. 10 is true: 'If thou faint in the day of adversity [if you give up when things are difficult], thy strength is small [you are not much good]'. It is a poor fish that cannot swim against the stream.

(ii) *Feeling superior.* There are some verses in James which suggest other reasons for feeling superior besides those mentioned on page 210. The verses speak of Christians who despised others because they were not well dressed—perhaps (though this is not said) even in 'church'. Such feelings are not unknown today. Some people feel superior about the colour of their skins—as if God preferred white skins to brown or black! Others feel superior to those who seem to them old-fashioned. 'Yes, my grandfather went to church twice on Sunday, but that was ages back. We have other things to do.'

All the same, every Christian really knows that to stay away from church because one feels superior is not Christian conduct.

(iii) *Dull services.* Perhaps the first Jewish Christians thought Christian meetings dull compared with the services and ceremonies of the Temple. Certainly young modern Christians, used to the pictures and to motor-cycle rallies, do not find church services exciting or even, always, pleasant. 'The singing is bad.' 'The harmonium is wheezy.' 'The place is full of draughts.' 'The reader sniffs.' 'Our minister can't preach for nuts.' 'Church services are beastly dull.'

Obviously, the grumbles of early Jewish Christians and modern Christians are not in the same words. But both of them, perhaps, are making the same mistake. They are confusing outside with inside things. Good singing, dignified buildings, stately ceremonies: all these are often helps to worship, but they are outside things. Real worship is an inside thing. Who knows whether the woman with the cracked voice in the pew behind may not be praising God better than the trained choir-boy, or even than oneself?

Of course a cracked voice or a draughty seat is trying (it might be possible to choose a different place next Sunday). But to be put off by things like that from going to worship God seems sillier—much—than to refuse a drink of tea from a thick, ugly cup. Besides, not every-thing is tiresome every Sunday. Most often it is possible to find something good:

> Do not grudge
> To pick out treasure from an earthen pot.

The poet-clergyman who wrote that advice three hundred years ago—remembering, perhaps, that he too had sometimes preached badly—added a wise remark about dull sermons:

> . . . if all want [is without] sense,
> God takes a text, and preacheth patience [read 'patience' as three syllables].

The next three points are not mentioned in the New Testament as reasons for avoiding church, but they are certainly not new.

(iv) *Dislike of rules.* Some people say, 'I don't mind going to church when I feel like it or on a wet Sunday. But why should I be tied?' (You might ask them, 'Why should anyone be tied to do a duty?')

Dislike of rules is nothing new. But everyone who goes to a good school has learnt that they are useful. So has everyone who has played in a team game. People cannot work or play in groups without rules of one kind or another. Besides, obedience to rules leads to good habits, and without good habits life would be much too complicated. Children are taught good habits by good rules. Older boys and girls, like grown-up people, can make many of the rules they will follow for themselves.

A firm, straightforward rule about going to church every Sunday takes away the need for thinking, 'Shall I? Shan't I?' every time one feels disinclined, or a friend looks in wanting a companion for a walk. Soon, too, the friend gives up coming; he knows it will be no use. A rule is a protection against moods; against being pestered, and against one's own excuses. It is no use being soft with oneself. No-one wants to grow up weak-kneed or without a backbone.

(v), (vi) *Love of pleasure; love of work.* These two reasons (excuses?) for not going to church seem contradictory, but both may be put forward from one cause. Neither love of pleasure nor love of work is bad in itself. Either may prevent a man or woman from attending church because he or she counts it matters more—say, on Sunday morning—than does his Christian duty. In the Middle Ages, some men were scolded or punished for 'hunting with dogs' in service time; some women were scolded or punished because they did their washing instead of going to church. Men and women are not punished for such reasons now. Christians must use their common sense in making their own rules, and their own steadiness in keeping them.

(vii) '*Services and sermons are hard to understand.*' Boys and girls of school-leaving age, if they are not practised in church-going, often give this reason for staying away. But they are not children. If they want to, they can learn.

One way of learning is to get to know church buildings well. Most English parish churches are open in daytime, and even people who do not belong to the Church of England can go in on a weekday and wander quietly round. They will see the pulpit for preaching; the lectern holding the Bible from which 'lessons'—chosen parts—are read; the organ and the choir seats which suggest the importance of singing; footstools for praying; the clergyman's place, from which he leads the services called Morning and Evening Prayer; the font for baptism; and, of course, the table or altar where the bread and wine are consecrated for the Eucharist (Holy Communion), and in front of that the rails where people kneel. In churches of other denominations such things are differently arranged, but in one form or another they will nearly all be there.

Another way of learning how to join in services, and what they mean, is for a boy or girl to take with him to church a friend who does not usually go. Anyone who does that begins at once to think how he can explain. Then it seems worth while to find out what he does not know himself. (Often boys and girls who do not go

Things seen in churches

On the altar, at the east end of the chancel, a cross usually stands

would like to, if only someone of their own age, or just a little older, would invite them.) Anyhow, if several people go together, they will discuss the service afterwards, and in that way begin to understand. Together they can ask someone for explanations, a thing they might not like to do alone.

It is worth remembering, too, that in nearly all churches preachers make their sermons more difficult or easy according to the congregation. If they see that young people come regularly, they explain more fully and in a more interesting way; if Sunday after Sunday only older people come to church, naturally the minister will preach for them alone. Very likely, too, more hymns will be chosen of the kind that boys and girls enjoy, and everyone will like to hear them singing.

Sometimes younger people feel that a congregation is unfriendly. 'In my church', a boy or girl may say, 'everyone is so stand-offish.' Perhaps he or she forgets that older people, as well as younger, may be shy; a grown-up person may decide not to smile or speak for fear a boy or girl should think him patronizing. Anyhow, people who stay away because others seem unfriendly is not doing much to increase friendliness!

Of course, Christians do not go to church just for the sake of being together. They go because God meets them there. He comes to them in other places too, and when they are alone. As a Jewish prophet taught, God does not dwell only in the 'high and holy place'—the Temple (or the church) set apart for him—but with each man who truly wants to learn. But people who never pray or sing together in church are likely, before long, to give up saying their prayers alone. God has made us to help each other, even in our worship of him.

To worship God is the chief reason why Christians go to church. And if someone says, 'I do not really know what that means', the answer is this: 'The meaning of worship, like loving, is learned as you try to do it'.

God meets people who want to meet him—want to enough to take the trouble of coming together in church. Quite soon they will probably discover that to have met God in church makes a difference in ordinary life. Everyone knows the difference it makes to meet and talk with a friend, especially if one is feeling 'down'. People who go regularly to church may find that they have had an experience rather like that. And everyone feels down sometimes.

Even the youths shall faint and be weary, and the young men shall utterly fall:

But they that wait upon the Lord shall renew their strength; they shall mount up with wings as eagles; they shall run, and not be weary; and they shall walk, and not faint.

CHAPTER XXVI

The puzzle of life after death

For study

The end of a conversation

John iv. 21-26

Whether in life or death . . .

1 Thessalonians v, 9-11

Romans xiv. 7-9

A sure promise

John xiv. 1-6

For extra reading

The present, and the end

1 Thessalonians iv. 11-18

In or out of the body

2 Corinthians v. 6-10

THE boy was four. With a grown-up friend he went to visit a house where a parrot lived. 'Please', said the boy when they got there, 'may we see the parrot?' The lady of the house looked sad. 'You cannot see the parrot,' she said, 'the parrot is dead.' 'Oh dear!' said the friend. The boy said: 'Where *is* the parrot?' The lady answered: 'The parrot is dead'. 'But where *is* the parrot?' repeated the boy, and his eyes were big. For a moment the lady was silent. Then she looked at the boy. 'The parrot has gone to heaven', she said. So the boy and his friend went away.

The parrot's owner had hesitated because she did not know what was true. The parrot's body was buried in the garden. But was that the whole of the parrot? Was any part of the bird which had been her companion for years still alive? She could not say.

Some people think that the animals they are fond of are not all body. Almost everyone, perhaps, has known a dog, or a cat, or a horse, who was such a friend that it is hard to believe it has been, so to speak, blown out like a candle at death. Such animals, perhaps, do come to share in something akin to the inside life of human beings. But there is no proof, and the Bible does not tell us. There are, however, some verses in Paul's Epistle to the Romans which speak of the hope that 'nature in its turn will be set free . . . to share in the glorious freedom of God's sons' (so Knox translates part of Romans viii. 21).

It is different with people. The poem about creation at the beginning of the Bible which we call the first chapter of Genesis, says that God created men and women in his own image. He made them to be his friends. The whole of the Bible is really talking about the possibility of friendship between God and human beings.

Now Jesus taught that God is Spirit, and that his worshippers must worship him in spirit and in truth (the Authorized Version of John iv. 24 says 'God is a Spirit', but the meaning is best understood if the 'a' is left out). People could not worship God if they were only bodies. It is their spirits which reach out to him, their very inmost selves. They reach out also with their minds, trying to worship him by thinking and behaving honestly. Animals were not created in God's image. We are not taught that they can worship him in spirit and in truth.

It is because men and women can be friends with God that we believe in 'heaven' for such people when they die. The owner of the parrot would not have hesitated to tell the boy that a child had 'gone to heaven'. Yet even then his question would not have had an answer in the sense the boy meant. Heaven is where God is; but God is not a place. In another way, too, the answer might give a wrong idea. God is with a child when he is living—and, of course, with grown-up people too, unless they do not want to be his friends. If we say that someone who has died has 'gone to heaven' we do not mean that he is now with God for the first time; we mean that his spirit is more free than when his body was alive to meet God who is Spirit. But still the question is not answered, 'What happens to us when we die?'

We know what happens to our bodies. They are buried, or cremated. Burial was the custom followed by the Jews, and by nearly all Christians until, roughly, the present century. It is still, in Britain, the most usual custom, but anyone who wishes can arrange that his body shall be cremated. It is a matter of choice or of convenience. Either way, our bodies, which are no longer needed, are destroyed. The method of destruction makes no difference to Christian belief in the resurrection of the body; that is not concerned with the particles of matter which make up what may be called the clothes worn by our spirits now (look back to pages 97, 144). The question is, What happens to *us* when we die? that is, What happens to our spirits—our inmost selves, when we leave our 'clothes' behind to be destroyed?

Some people think that after death our spirits are asleep until the day of resurrection. The Jews sometimes spoke of death as sleep, and in the New Testament the symbol is often used. The first Christians liked it; they were no more afraid of death than they were of going to sleep. Other people think that that picture-word suggests something too much like the idea of the old woman who is said to have wanted this epitaph put upon her tombstone:

Don't mourn for me now, don't mourn for me never:
I'm going to do nothing for ever and ever.

Such people think that 'sleep' is a good word to use about our bodies, but not about our spirits. They believe that if death means going to be with God, his friends will be more active when they have left their worn-out clothes behind than the word sleep implies.

Three special questions have been asked by boys and girls about what happens to us when we die.

(1) *Do the spirits of dead people come to talk to us?* To put it the other way round: *When we are dead, shall we be able*

to talk to people still living in their bodies? The people who are known as Spiritualists say, Yes. Spiritualists believe that through mediums conversations can be carried on between the living and the dead. A medium is a man or woman who can go into a trance, a state in which he or she is cut off for a time from ordinary life and 'tuned in', so to speak, to a world of spirits. The medium, so Spiritualists believe, can then learn from the spirits what cannot be known in ordinary ways, and can pass the knowledge back to ordinary people.

Readers of *Servants of God at Work* will remember that King Saul once went to a witch and asked her to get into touch with the spirit of the prophet Samuel. The witch would, in modern times, have been called a medium. She, and the king, believed that Samuel's spirit appeared, and spoke. That experience, as readers know, did Saul no good.

The Old Testament again and again forbids men to go to fortune-tellers, or magicians, or other people who believe themselves to be in touch with spirits. In the book of the prophet Isaiah there is a verse which tells God's servants not to listen to those who advise them to consult wizards 'that peep, and that mutter' (Authorized Version), that is, 'who talk in ghostly voices over their enchantments' (Knox). God's servants must do what he has taught them—taught them in straightforward ways.

In the New Testament 'witchcraft'—trying to talk with and use spirits—comes in a list of sins which matter very much. Its place is between idolatry and hatred.

The Bible does not say that spirits—the spirits of people who have died, or other spirits—cannot come to talk with us. It says that trying to talk with them does not help us to serve God.

People who go to séances (private meetings) or to public meetings where mediums are at work easily get out of touch with ordinary life. They may come to feel themselves special in some way—superior, perhaps, to other people. Sometimes they become so much taken up with the idea of getting help and comfort for themselves that they are less nice to live with; they give less thought and time to serving God by helping other people. Perhaps they are selfish towards the spirits too. Christians may think that their friends who have died have something better to do than to answer questions—often unimportant questions—put to them by mediums. It is possible—we do not know—that those who try to make spirits talk are holding them back, as a child might be kept back from going into a higher class.

(2) *Is it true that after we die we come back as something different?* About this question four things may be said. (*a*) The Bible gives no teaching on the subject. (*b*) No clear reasons for believing in the theory have been found by people who learn only in ordinary ways, through science, say, or history, or experience. Only those who are in some sense or another Spiritualists feel sure that the theory is true. (*c*) The theory does not seem to fit in with the general teaching of the Bible, or with ordinary knowledge. (*d*) As no-one, except some kind of Spiritualist, thinks that he (or she) knows what he was in any earlier life or lives, or believes that he has memories from any, the theory does not seem to matter very much for ordinary, practical people.

(3) *Does such a place as Purgatory exist?* There is no direct teaching in the Bible about Purgatory. Neither

the Church of England nor any of the Free Churches say that Christians must believe in it. This is one of the points about which the teaching of the Roman Catholic Church is different. It believes that the spirits of Christians who die pass on to a state in which by suffering they are made more ready for the vision of God. Some Christians who are not Roman Catholics also believe this.

This chapter is nearly finished. Perhaps readers feel that it has said very little in answer to the question at its beginning. Indeed, the Bible tells us very little. All the same, some things are clear, and they are things that matter.

First, the early Christians were not afraid of dying. Paul wrote that if he could choose between living and dying he would not know what to say. He wanted to stay in his body because he thought that his friends needed his help. He wanted to die, because he would be with Christ—'a better thing, much more than a better thing', as a modern translation of the New Testament puts the verse (Philippians i. 23). In one of his earliest Epistles—1 Thessalonians—Paul wrote that Jesus Christ died for us so that waking in life or sleeping in death we should live together with him. Therefore, he said, go on encouraging one another and building up one another's faith.

In the Authorized Version, where you may be reading the verses in the second group set *For study*, you will find the word 'comfort' instead of 'encourage', but the translations which use 'encourage' give Paul's meaning more clearly for us. 'Edify' means 'building up'.

Secondly, the reason why the early Christians were not afraid to die is clear. You have read it here already in both the last two quotations from the New Testament. It was stated by Jesus himself in the last long talk he had with his disciples before his death. But do not look at the verses—the third group set *For study*—until you have read the story in the next paragraphs. It is taken (with leave) from a novel, but I think it is true.

Two young boys, called Jimmy and Montagu, were brothers. One day there was an accident and Jimmy died. A visitor who came to see Montagu used a phrase about death which is sometimes said without much thought: 'Jimmy is going home'. Montagu was puzzled. 'Not home like this,' he said doubtfully, 'not like *The Moorings*' (that was the name of his house). But suddenly his face cleared. 'I know,' he said, 'you mean "home" like home in hide-and-seek.' This time the visitor was puzzled. Then—'Yes,' he answered, 'it's perfectly true—like "home" in hide-and-seek—the place where you're absolutely safe.'

Now read the verses set *For study* from John xiv. If you could use the translation of Monsignor Knox you would see that the word given in verses 2 and 3 instead of 'place' is 'home'. Jesus, of course, was speaking to men who were his friends. He said that he was going to get ready a home where they would be with him—absolutely safe.

On the list lying on the writer's desk of questions about life after death which boys or girls in secondary schools have asked, one still remains: *What happens to the babies who are born and live only a few hours?*

Behind this question, two others may perhaps have lain.

(i) Do babies go on growing up somewhere else? For a suggestion about this, readers should again see page

Jesus lives! thy terrors now
  Can no more, O death, appal us;
Jesus lives! by this we know
  Thou, O grave, canst not enthral us
Alleluia

From an Easter hymn

'enthral' here means 'hold captive'

97. Age is something which belongs to bodies, not to spirits. Anyone who has had much to do with very young children will tell you that no two are just alike. Each is a small human being in his own right, a person. It is the spirit of that person—so Christians believe—that goes on if the baby's body dies.

(ii) Does it matter that the baby has had no chance of being taught? This is a question answered quite firmly by a woman who had seen many little children die. In one of her books she wrote: 'There is nothing ever to fear for [them]'.

But, some reader may ask, how did she know? Amy Carmichael, for it was she (*Servants of God at Work* tells of her), would have answered with two points.

First, she was quite sure that God is love, and that Jesus Christ, who told his disciples to let small children come to him, would not leave them uncared for after death. She believed what the writer of a hymn believed, a hymn which many boys and girls learn when they are little, the one beginning like this:

> Christ, who once amongst us
>   As a child did dwell,
> Is the children's Saviour
>   And he loves us well.

The last verse but one of that hymn speaks of life after death in symbols which express what Amy Carmichael believed is true for young children. Other real Christians are sure about it too:

> He [Jesus] will be our Shepherd
>   After as before,
> By still heavenly waters
>   Lead us evermore;

Make us lie in pastures
  Beautiful and green,
Where none thirst or hunger,
  And no tears are seen.

Secondly, Amy would have said she knew because she had watched many babies die. She wrote, quite seriously, about the 'other-world' look she had seen in their eyes. She tells stories about little children who were happy as they died. One, who was five, smiled and clapped her hands, 'as children do when welcoming someone whom they love', then held out her arms towards—?: the people round her could not see. Another, about two, a short time before she died smiled and tried to clap her hands in the familiar way she always did when she heard music. A third, Lala, aged five, was not with Amy when she died; her father, who was not a Christian, had taken her away. A non-Christian woman who had been near when she was very ill told what she had heard. Lala 'said she was Jesus' child, and did not seem afraid. And she said that she saw three Shining Ones come into the room where she was lying, and she was comforted.'

Once more, it is a paradox which for Christians is the 'answer' to a puzzle, this time the puzzle of life after death. They say that they do not know—and that they are quite sure.

CHAPTER XXVII

The puzzle of responsibility

For study

What lasts

1 Corinthians xiii. 4-13

Patience with each other

Romans xv. 1-6

For extra reading

Body and spirit belong to God

1 Corinthians vi. 19, 20

Husbands and wives

Ephesians v. 17, 20-33

Why can't you get married in church if you've been divorced?

WHY, to begin with, do young men and women want to get married in church? That is a question worth thinking about.

There is, of course, a legal answer. Marriages in church are recognized by the law of the land as a proper means by which a man and a woman become husband and wife. They and their children will have all the rights which belong to married people and their families as British citizens. But church marriages are not the only kind of marriages which the law of our land allows. Marriages according to certain recognized forms and in front of recognized officials are also legal. From the point of view of the law of the land—of the state, as people say—marriage in a registry office in the presence of the official known as the Registrar, is just as good as marriage in church. So the legal answer to the question, 'Why do people want to be married in church?' is not really an answer at all. It only echoes the question, Why should they?

Secondly, there is a social answer. A marriage in church means, if you wish, a certain amount of fuss. The building is well known; there are, perhaps, bells to be rung; there is space for plenty of guests, and even for mere lookers-on: a church wedding makes the bride and bridegroom feel important.

Thirdly, there is what might be called the sartorial answer—only the word is so ugly; it means, the answer which has to do with clothes. Every girl wants to look nice on her wedding-day, and so, for that matter, does a man—though as he is usually happiest in his oldest jacket, he takes this point in a different way. The normal man naturally wants his bride to look her best, and at bottom he is pleased that she should have bridesmaids to do her honour. Flowers and pretty dresses make a good background on what truly is a special occasion.

The social and the sartorial answers to the question 'Why do people want to get married in church?' are not silly answers. But they do not go very deep. First, they are unsatisfactory because weddings in registry offices need not be so dull as they seem; a change in social customs might come about. Secondly, these two reasons why the outside of a church wedding may be good cannot really stand alone: the outside is a symbol of something inside. A wedding, as was said at the end of the last paragraph, truly is a special occasion. Anyone who stops at the attractive outside reasons for wanting to be married in church has not got far. Confetti is swept up, and flowers fade, and before long there are Monday mornings again. The memory of a pretty wedding is pleasant, but it can't take the weight of everyday married life.

The fourth answer to the question is religious. Christians want to get married in church because a wedding is so very important. The inside thing—the joining of two lives—is more important than anything else in the relations of people to each other. Men and women who believe in God and try every day to behave as Jesus taught, know that without God they are not able to please him. They would not dare to make such solemn promises as people who marry make to each other except in his presence, and with the certainty of his help.

Of course other Christian groups as well as the Church of England have their own forms of religious service for the marriage of their members. The normal thing is for people to be married with the service used by their own group. This chapter, however, is written in answer to a question about being married in a church of the Church of England. The rule against the marriage of a divorced person in church is a Church of England rule. The promises of which the chapter is going to tell are taken from the service printed in the Book of Common Prayer. Many clergymen of the Church of England use some prayers which are easier to understand than the printed ones, but the promises are not changed. In other religious groups promises of the same kind are made. The rest of this chapter expresses Christian thought in general, though it uses Anglican (Church of England) language.

The Prayer Book service shows clearly how solemn are the promises made at a wedding. First comes the answer to the question which the clergyman asks the man and the woman separately. It is exactly the same for each, with only the necessary change from 'her' to 'him'. Each, separately, answers 'I will'. (The word 'thou' is used because it is in the singular; we now use 'you' for both singular and plural, but the old-fashioned 'thou' in the question seems to emphasize that it is said to one person only at a time.)

Wilt thou . . . forsaking all other[s], keep thee only unto her (him) so long as ye [you] both shall live?

No-one can honestly say 'I will' in answer to that question if he or she is thinking, 'But, of course, if things go wrong, I can get a divorce'. The promise is for better

for worse,

for richer

for poorer,

in sickness

and in health . . .

till death us do part

made before God. A little later the man puts the ring on the woman's finger, and as he does so he says:

> With this ring I thee wed. . . . In the Name of the Father, and of the Son, and of the Holy Ghost.

Before this point in the service is reached, the man and the woman make more detailed promises to each other. Each uses the same words, with one exception:

> I [So-and-so], take thee [So-and-so], to my wedded wife (husband), to have and to hold [keep] from this day forward . . . for better for worse, for richer for poorer, in sickness and in health . . . till death us do part.

'In sickness and in health.' That sounds easy enough when a man and a woman are young and neither, perhaps, has known much more about illness than the discomfort of slight influenza. But what if one of them has an accident which means weeks in bed, or perhaps blindness or a wheel-chair for the rest of his or her life? Can the other face that?

'For richer for poorer.' 'Well, we are not afraid of work, and we needn't buy a washing machine till next year.' But suppose, through no fault of either, jobs become scarce; or as the family increases the prices of food and clothes go up; and there is no money for holidays, and even tickets for the pictures, and the TV licence, can't be afforded: what then? Is the wife going to mind so much that she drives the man into gambling in the hope of gaining money (though, in fact, he is a great deal more likely to lose it)? Is the man going to nag because his wife is less smart and the meals are less good, till she gives up trying?

More difficult still, 'For better for worse'. No two people before marriage know all about each other. It is one thing to look forward to week-ends and to grudge every half-hour of free time which cannot be spent in each other's company. It is a different thing to face the commonplace details of ordinary life together, month after month, year after year. What about those annoying small habits? What about the need to be ready, all the time, to fit in with someone elses wishes and fads? (The promises, remember, are in general the same for each.) What about the bad temper, or the managing ways, or the greediness, which before marriage did not show?

Readers who look forward to having, one day, a wedding in church, must think what the promises made there will mean. The only point in the Prayer Book service on which they differ for the man and the woman is that the woman says she will 'obey' her husband. That word was left out in a revised version of the service which was proposed some years ago, and some religious groups do not use it. Many people think that the woman should not be asked to make such a promise, because it puts her into a lower position than her husband. On the other hand, people who think that 'obey' should remain in the service believe that for a man to take the lead comes naturally out of the differences between men and women. The powers of the sexes are obviously not just the same, but that does not mean that one is more important than another. Differences, yes. Superiority, no.

The more thought that is given to the promises which a man and a woman make to each other in church, the more plainly an answer to the question at the head of this chapter begins to show itself. The rule that a divorced man or woman must not make those promises again while the first person to whom, in the presence of

God, he or she made them is still living, begins to seem a sensible, even perhaps a natural, rule.

But, says someone, suppose a husband or wife has broken a promise? Suppose he or she has committed adultery (see pages 118, 119), that is, has not 'kept only' to the partner, or has deserted him or her because the marriage has turned out 'for worse'? Is not the partner who is left behind acting rightly if he or she makes promises to someone else?

The law of the land allows people whose marriages have been broken by, for example, adultery, to be divorced. The marriage may be brought to an end in a court of law, and then they are free to marry again. Either partner can make new promises to someone else in a registry office; a new marriage is legal, and the new couple's children will have full legal rights.

The leaders of the Church of England know that a marriage which has taken place in a church may fail. They know that the promises made there may be broken, even by men and women who really meant to keep them. They do not say that divorced people can never again count as full members of the Church. But they know also that a man and a woman married in church promised to hold to each other 'for better for worse . . . till death us do part'. If they allowed those vows to be taken again, even if the man or woman who wants to take them is not the person to blame for the failure of the first marriage, it would make the promises seem less solemn. People might feel that, after all, divorce does not matter too much; that a vow made before God is not so very important. It is not a question of punishment. It is a question of standing for the true meaning of Christian marriage.

Perhaps someone thinks, 'If a church wedding means so much, I shan't want to have one'. But a young man and woman who really care for each other do not want their marriage to break. If they are Christians they will surely be glad to make vows to each other in God's sight. They will be glad to know that the people in church are praying for them, asking God to help them to keep their promises and to build a happy new home. This, of course, is true whether 'church' in the last sentence means a parish church, which is Church of England, or the building used for worship by some other Christian group. If a member of another Christian group wants to be married in a church of the Church of England, the couple must consult the rector or vicar of the parish.

If a man and woman are not Christians and yet want to be married in church, it will probably be for one of the first three reasons mentioned on pages 231, 232. The second and third reasons are not enough to make it right for them to go through a solemn Christian service. The first reason is a reason for a legal but not for a Christian wedding. The marriage of two non-Christians should take place in a registry office.

Such a marriage also is a very serious ceremony: the promises are not meant to be broken. If the marriage breaks down, a divorce can only be obtained for the same reasons as for a marriage in church, and the case will be heard in the same kind of law court. The law of the land is the same for everyone, Christian or not. It is not the business of the state—that is, the law and government of a country—to insist on Christian marriage. (This does not mean that people who work for the state—judges, members of parliament, civil servants and so on—may not be Christians themselves: they often are.) The state's business is to protect its citizens and to try to bring about good public behaviour. It must as far as it can make sure that couples are legally married and do not bring into the world children who will have no legal rights. If a marriage in a registry office is legally ended by a divorce, a man or woman is free to be married again in the same way as before.

Marriages do not 'turn out well' by chance. It is not enough that a bride and bridegroom feel themselves madly in love. Two people who start out with dreams of a perpetual good time will soon find that they have made a mistake. They need a sense of responsibility towards each other and towards their promises. If they are Christians, they will feel a sense of responsibility towards God for each other and for their children.

To keep the promises made in marriage means unselfishness and self-control. It means willingness to lose one's life in order to save it. That is a Christian paradox, and it cannot be fully put into practice without the grace of God. But God's grace is there for every Christian who wants it and, as Paul knew, that grace is enough, whatever the circumstances of a life may be. Thousands of happily married people could tell you that they have found that true.

CHAPTER XXVIII

Some puzzles of prayer

For study

Prayers to Jesus for help

Matthew xv. 21-28

Mark iv. 35-41

Luke xviii. 35-43

Jesus teaches about prayer

Matthew vi. 5-9

For extra reading

Divisions of prayer

Asking

Matt. xviii. 19, 20; John xiv. 13-15

Thanking

1 Thess. v. 18; Col. iii. 17

Confession

1 John i. 5-9; Psalm li. 1-3, 10

Prayer for others

Luke viii. 41, 42, 49-56; Eph. iii. 14-16

Praise

Psalm cxlv. 1-12; cxlviii. 1-14

How do we know that God is really there?

Is there a scientific explanation to all the miracles [*in the Gospels*], *and does this undermine the power of Jesus?*

TEACHERS of the Christian religion in school, in church, or anywhere else, talk about prayer. So does the Bible, in both the Old and New Testaments. So did Jesus.

But what does prayer mean? Why do Christian mothers teach small children to say their prayers? Why do so many grown-up people leave off saying them? What, after all, is prayer?

Readers of the four books of *Roads to Christian Faith* know that a great many Christian beliefs can best be explained by symbols. The picture on the next page shows a symbol for prayer which no-one who died more than about a hundred years ago could have thought of (why?). It is, of course, only a symbol, and it suggests only some points about prayer: readers might here stop and jot down any they can think of—if their minds are blank, they can at least draw the symbol!

What is a telephone for? It is something by which a man or woman can talk with somebody out of sight. It makes possible the interchange of ideas at a distance. It is what is called a means of communication. Any of these points on readers' lists might be ticked.

Prayer is a means of communication between God and human beings. Like a telephone, it gives opportunities for conversations, not just for one-sided remarks. A telephone talk between friends is next best to a meeting face to face. God himself speaks with men who pray,

A symbol
Of what? a good or bad one?

though 'his dwelling is in unapproachable light' and no human eye has seen or can ever see him (look back to page 23). It is said in the book of Exodus that when Moses prayed God spoke to him 'as a man speaks to his friend'.

No-one can pray unless he thinks that God is, or at least may be, there. 'How are they [people] to call upon him until they have learned to believe in him?' asks Paul in his Epistle to the Romans (x. 14). 'Nobody', says the writer of Hebrews (xi. 6), 'reaches God's presence until he has learned to believe that God exists, and that he rewards those who try to find him.' The second sentence of that verse from Hebrews speaks of a second thing which the man who prays must believe. It is that communication between God and human beings is possible. To believe in God without believing that there is a way by which people may be in touch with him does not take anyone very far.

To believe in God to some people seems very difficult, though to others, not to believe that he is there seems more difficult still. (Look again at pages 22 and 23 of this book.) And here is one of the paradoxes of prayer: you cannot pray unless you first think that God is there —though you may want to put in a 'perhaps'; yet it is by praying that you may become quite sure he is—and learn to cross 'perhaps' firmly out. Readers may guess how the telephone may be a symbol on this point too.

Some things which are said about prayer are difficult to understand because the word is used in a sense different from the ordinary one. It may mean not actually talking with God but just readiness for a conversation. A child playing in a room where someone he trusts is, say, reading a newspaper, does not think about or talk to that person all the time. He thinks about his toys, but underneath he knows that he can at any minute ask for help, or just call out, 'Oh, look!' Anyone who is learning, say, to swim, or to drive a car, likes to know that a teacher in whom he has confidence is at hand, though he may not think about him unless he wants to ask a question. In the same way, there is a kind of prayer which is an underneath knowledge that God is there, though the person who trusts him may be thinking about ordinary work or play.

When Paul in his First Epistle to the Thessalonians (v. 17) wrote, 'Pray without ceasing', he clearly did not mean, 'Spend all your time saying prayers'. He may have meant, 'Never give up prayer'; or perhaps he was using 'pray' in the less common sense. Perhaps he wanted the Christians to whom he was writing to be always ready to answer the telephone if God should ring. (Of course Paul did not use that symbol!)

Most people begin to find what it means to have conversations with God by learning to say their prayers—to ring him up, so to speak—at special times and in special words. That is why Christian parents teach their children to say very simple prayers. Yet some people make such prayers an excuse for giving up prayer when they are older. They feel that it is foolish to go on speaking to God in baby language; and so it is. No man or woman talks with his or her friends as he did as a child. Both he and the friends have changed. God does not change: 'with [him] is no variableness' (James i. 17). But as people grow up they learn more about him, and their prayers should grow up too.

Boys and girls might find that their own prayers would grow up if they kept a private note-book in which to put down what they want to say to God. They could write headings or subjects for prayers, or make up short prayers of their own. (It is not length that matters—Jesus said so.) They could put in prayers from the New Testament, such as the request of the woman in the story set in the first group of verses *For study*. They could copy some of the 'collects' (prayers on a special subject, a few sentences long) from a Church of England Prayer Book; examples of collects which any Christian can use are given on pages 48 and 197 of this book. They could choose and write out verses from hymns.

There is one prayer taught to children which need not be left behind as they grow up. That is the prayer which Jesus gave his disciples. Children often learn it when they can understand hardly any of the sentences (which do readers still consider difficult?). Later, if they think about the meaning, they will find that that grows and grows. Someone once said that the Lord's Prayer is like the sea: a child may paddle at the edge of the water, but further out a strong man must swim.

About thirty years ago a discovery was made which showed that the Lord's Prayer was known in Britain seventeen hundred years ago, when the country was part of the Roman Empire. The discovery was the answer to the puzzle shown in the frontispiece of this book.

The piece of red plaster which is drawn at the top of the page was found in the remains of the wall of a house in Cirencester. The house was built when Romans lived in the town in the third century or even earlier. It was found getting on for a hundred years ago, but for about sixty years no-one could spell out words that made good sense. Then a learned man saw that the letters could be arranged as they are on the lower part of the frontispiece. So arranged (without the A's and O's beyond the little lines at the four ends of the cross) they make the words PATER NOSTER, from top to bottom and from left to right. 'Pater' is Latin for 'father', and 'noster' for 'our'. Readers will be able to guess what 'A' and 'O' symbolize. Like the monogram in Greek letters on the cover of this book, they stand for *alpha* and *omega*, the first and last letters of the Greek alphabet, and are used as a symbol of Jesus. So the mixed-up letters make the first words of the prayer which Jesus taught.

The arrangement of the letters in the answer to the puzzle was used in other towns in the Roman Empire besides Cirencester. It has been found twice over in Pompeii, the city in Italy which was destroyed by an eruption of Mount Vesuvius in A.D. 79, less than twenty years, probably, after Paul and Peter died. It may have been used by Christians as a kind of private message to each other, especially in times of persecution. Readers who keep a private book for prayers might copy on its first page the Paternoster cross with the A's and O's. It will remind them that Christians, who pray in the name of Jesus, have always used the prayer which he taught.

Some boys and girls who are growing up stop saying their prayers not because the prayers are childish but because it seems childish to pray at all. They feel like people who have just passed their driving test; they want, so to speak, to take the 'L' off their cars and manage alone. Perhaps for a time they can. But living is much more difficult than driving, and it needs more courage as well as more time to learn. Besides, Christians do not pray only because they need God's help; a telephone is not made to be used from one end only.

The story in Genesis pictures God walking with Adam and Eve as his friends 'in the cool of the day'. But they disobeyed him, and had to leave the Garden. That is a parable of how men and women choose their own way and refuse the friendship of God. Yet God still wants to speak to them; Jesus died that their sins might be forgiven. Anyone who decides to stop saying his prayers because he does not want to be in touch with God forgets that God may 'ring him up'. But, of course, if he refuses to answer the bell he will presently cease to hear it, however often it rings.

A third reason why people give up praying is that they no longer believe that God is there. On this question readers should again look back to pages 22 to 28. They should remember, too, that even real Christians sometimes feel that there is no answer when they try to use their telephone; the line seems to be dead. Then it is no use despairing, or getting excited as the prophets of the false god Baal did in Elijah's time—the men who 'cried aloud and cut themselves after their manner with knives'. God's servants must go on with their prayers as usual, even when they have to begin by saying, 'O God, if you are there . . .'. Presently they will find that they can leave out the 'if' sentence: the line will be clear again.

A fourth reason why people stop praying is that they have not let their ideas about God grow bigger as they grew up. Perhaps they thoughtlessly picture him as the kind of father who spoils a boy, or as like one who does not recognize that his son or daughter is no longer a child. Or perhaps they feel that God is somehow too small for a world about which scientists know so much more than anyone knew even a few years ago, almost as though God—the Creator—had not yet caught up with modern discoveries! Or they may say, 'People who pray ask God to do miracles. Miracles can't happen. I'm not going to kid myself that they can.'

The girl who asked the second question printed at the top of this chapter was puzzled about the miracles described in the Gospels. Her puzzle was part of the bigger problem, Can miracles happen at all?

The first point to consider is, What is a miracle? Here readers might write down their own ideas.

A miracle is an event which cannot be explained by any causes known to men. A miracle appears to be contradictory to the habits of things, that is, to the 'laws' (ordinary customs) according to which God usually works, and men work too. But it is impossible to draw a fixed line between miracles and 'not-miracles', because men never come to the end of learning the 'laws' of things; as they find out more, events which were once called miracles may be seen to be examples of newly discovered laws.

There is now a scientific explanation for some—not all—of the 'miracles' told of in the Gospels. Yet if science one day explains them all, that will not alter what Christians believe about Jesus. He did not work miracles to make people see he was someone special. He worked them, almost always, in answer to a prayer for help. He worked them by the power of God, and by that same power his disciples could sometimes work them too.

Jesus was always in touch with God, his Father. Not once did he choose to do what he himself wanted instead of what God wanted; not once did he care more about himself than about other people. So, through him, the power of God could always be used to help people. Often, as has just been said, he used a scientific law. At other times he did something which still seems contradictory to the habits of things. Perhaps those things were according to a law men will one day learn. But perhaps God sometimes chose, and chooses, to make exceptions. Some modern scientists say that even in science allowance must be made for exceptions, though others say that what look like exceptions will one day be seen to fit in with a law or laws not yet discovered. The more men find out about God's world, the more they find out how little they know.

No-one has come to the end of learning about God's power. But there is one thing he cannot do. He cannot be untrue to himself. He cannot give up caring for people, even when they do not care about him.

Of course God does not give people everything they ask for when they pray. Anyone, like Amy Carmichael, may have to take 'No' for an answer (if you can, see *Servants of God at Work*). But everyone, young or old, who wants to be in touch with God may be quite natural when he or she prays. It is for God to decide what, and when, and how, he answers.

A mother once told a child he might ask God for anything. When the boy prayed that a railway tunnel which had frightened him might be taken away, she was startled. But next time the boy had to travel on that line he went to sleep before the train reached the tunnel, and only woke up when it had passed it. So for him, that day, there was no tunnel at all. Was that a miracle? or not? Anyhow, I hope the boy remembered to thank God for answering his prayer.

Prayer is not always asking: it cannot be, if it is a conversation with God, any more than can a talk between human friends. It may be thanking God, or telling him about other people's problems as well as one's own, or owning up to one's failures and sins, or just thinking about the wonderful things he does.

Readers who wish to put prayers in any of these divisions into their private books will find plenty in a hymn book. They might start by looking up in its Index hymns which begin with the word 'praise', and picking out from them a few verses or lines. Or they could choose words from Psalms such as xcv, ciii, cxlv, cxlviii.

Hymns and psalms are reminders of one very important paradox of prayer, though it is one into which the symbol of the telephone does not fit. Prayer is something in which each single Christian may, in a sense, be alone with God. But it is just as true that no Christian prays alone. He or she is always a member of the great host of God's servants. He belongs to the Church, the company of all faithful people, which Paul calls the Body of Jesus Christ who is its Head.

Any Christian may get discouraged about saying his prayers; but the prayer of the Church goes on. And if somebody asks, 'Is taking so hard a road worth while?'—

> Saints, apostles, prophets, martyrs,
> Answer, Yes.

Readers of *Roads to Christian Faith* know the names of people who belong to all these groups. Ordinary Christians who do not belong to any of them—Christian and Christiana of *Pilgrim's Progress*—say just the same.

For discussion

THE COLOUR BAR

(i) Are white people inferior to coloured?
Notes. Difference is not the same as superiority or inferiority.
Looks are not the same as character or personality.
Strangers are not the same as enemies.
What one likes is not the same as what is important.

(ii) Should white and coloured people intermarry?
Notes. Men and women of different races (*a*) think differently; (*b*) feel differently; (*c*) are likely to act differently in crises.
For centuries they have had (*a*) different backgrounds; (*b*) different customs; (*c*) different ways of looking at things.
Are these differences good or bad for (*a*) husband and wife; (*b*) the children, who in one family may be coloured, or white, or of mixed colour and mixed characteristics?

(iii) Should young people of different races spend their leisure time together?
Notes. Understanding between such people helps towards world peace.
Companionship prevents loneliness but (*a*) misunderstanding of each other's words and actions may be easy because unsuspected; (*b*) to go too far and draw back is hurtful.
Exciting pleasures, dancing especially, lead easily to loss of self-control.
Close friendships may take you further than you really wish.

(iv) In Galatians iii. 28 St. Paul writes:

> There is neither Jew nor Greek, there is neither bond nor free . . .: for ye are all one in Christ Jesus.

What has this to do with the colour bar?
What does Paul mean by 'ye are all one *in Christ Jesus*'?

For discussion

BIBLE READING

Should Christians read the Bible?

Each of the following remarks is true, untrue, or half true. Under which heading should each be put?

The Bible is: out of date
full of ideas worth thinking about
too hard to understand
only fit for Jews to read
full of dead history and imaginary stories
a book by which God speaks to men and women.

The Bible tells about: Jesus Christ
people who looked for God and found him
the Church and how it began.

The Bible shows: what Christians ought to do
how Jewish history prepared for Christ's coming
how Christians may learn to pray.

Choose the four most important reasons for Bible reading, and write them out in a tidy list. Discuss the lists.

Discuss the difficulties of regular Bible reading, such as:

(i) 'I'm too busy.' (Does this mean, 'I don't think it matters'?)
(ii) 'I don't know what to read.' (Could you join the Bible Reading Fellowship or the Scripture Union?)
(iii) 'I don't understand.' (The B.R.F. and S.U. publish notes to help.)
(iv) 'I forget.' (Many churches and clubs have discussion groups or classes; or friends can make a plan, and remind each other.)

Read John xv. 4, 5. Discuss why the reading is suggested.

For discussion

CIVIL MARRIAGE

Would it be good to make civil marriage (that is, marriage before a public official) compulsory? (Those who wished could arrange for a religious service also.)

Discuss these arguments: some are good, some are bad.

For. (1) Less opportunity for hypocrisy. People now often choose a religious service for non-religious reasons.

(2) Fewer people who were later divorced would have difficulties about re-marriage.

(3) Saving of money.

(4) Saving of time and fuss.

(5) The state (the country organized for government) would be treating all its citizens alike.

(6) Christians and non-Christians would both feel that their opinions about religion were respected.

Against. (1) Fewer religious marriages. 'Border-line' Christians (and non-Christians) who now choose religious marriages for non-religious reasons would lose (*a*) the dignity and solemnity of Christian marriage; (*b*) a special opportunity of thinking about the need and the possibility of God's help for a happy marriage.

(2) People might take divorce less seriously.

(3) The spending of time and money may be good because they make a marriage seem very important.

(4) The state is fair to all citizens while it counts both religious and civil marriage legal. 'Fairness' does not mean that everything must be exactly the same for everyone.

(5) To treat a religious service as an 'extra' might make people feel that religion does not much matter.

For discussion

PACIFISM

Is it wrong for Christians to join the Forces?

Some points to discuss:

Deliberately to kill or injure anyone is wrong.

War means killing and injury to non-combatants, including women, children, old people, pacifists.

Jesus Christ never used force to defend himself or his disciples.

Christians should not defend themselves by force; God often allows his servants to be martyrs.

Christians must fight against evil; there are evils (for example, to allow other people to be treated with cruelty) which may be worse than war.

War brings out the best in people.

War brings out the worst in people.

In the Forces, men and women accept pain and death for themselves to save other people from those evils and from worse evils (which would fall on themselves too).

Sometimes men must choose between a greater and a smaller evil; there may be no absolutely right action they could take.

If your country is at war, to refuse to help the 'war effort' may be disloyal.

If your country is at war, you cannot (except by leaving it, or going to prison) put yourself outside the war effort; everybody counts.

Christians live in the world: in peace, they must obey laws with which they disagree; in war they are still citizens—they still have duties to their country.

If there is contradiction between duty to God and duties to men, a Christian must at any cost obey God first.

INDEX

Roman figures refer to chapters. f., ff. *means 'following page, or pages'*

III

Prophets. Martyrs. The Church through the wo

II

Stories and Poetry. The Law and History.
Books of Symbols, and Letters.

I

The Life of Peter, Volumes I, II. The Life of Pa